Ten
Great Escapes

Hariharan Subramanian, the founder of Children Reunited, rescues, rehabilitates and reunites runaway children with their families. His organization has helped more than 30,000 runaway children—who land up in various railway stations in Maharashtra—escape exploitation.

Hari has also established free clinics for children in Kerala and Maharashtra and sponsors the skill development of around 4,000 children throughout India. He also set up Street Children Foundation. As a member of Children's Aid Society, Government of Maharashtra, he has been entrusted with the running of a boarding school for 150 children in Wada.

His philanthropic endeavours include distributing close to 1,000 free daily meals to guardians of patients at Thane Municipal Hospital, which has now been extended to include senior citizens and people who are blind, deaf and mute living alone in nearby areas.

Hari is planning to gradually add all major Indian railway stations for his rescue work and create public awareness towards reducing the number of runaways. His upcoming movie titled *Otta* (A Loner) with the Oscar-winning sound engineer Resul Pookutty at the helm is one such awareness initiative.

Born in Palakkad, he completed his MBA in Marketing and Finance from the University of Pune and launched a BPO—Pace Setters Business Solutions Pvt. Ltd.—which has a present headcount of more than 6,000 people.

His first book *Runaway Children* came out in 2015. *Ten Great Escapes* is his second non-fiction. Reach him on Instagram @childrenreunitedindia.

Ten Great Escapes

True Stories of
RUNAWAY CHILDREN

HARIHARAN S.

RUPA

Published by
Rupa Publications India Pvt. Ltd 2023
7/16, Ansari Road, Daryaganj
New Delhi 110002

Sales centres:
Bengaluru Chennai
Hyderabad Jaipur Kathmandu
Kolkata Mumbai Prayagraj

P-ISBN: 978-93-5702-947-6
E-ISBN: 978-93-5702-785-4

First impression 2023

10 9 8 7 6 5 4 3 2 1

Printed in India

Dedicated to
all runaway children
and
any child who's suffering

Contents

Foreword

I learned about Hariharan through my brother's friend, and from what I understood, he is a successful businessman who owns a BPO. But when he gave me a copy of his book *Runaway Children* on our first meeting, my views about him changed. I discovered that as a boy, he ran away from home three times, and his extreme life experiences inspired my first directorial venture *Otta* (A Loner).

As my interactions with Hariharan increased, I came to appreciate his greatness because, as a runaway child himself, he was able to relate to the problems of other runaways and had since helped rescue more than 30,000 children. Usually, people try to avoid the bad memories of the past, but Hariharan has taken it as a challenge to help all the children who are suffering.

Hariharan wants to tell us through this book how and why children end up being loners. He has selected ten instances to represent various issues faced by children—from why they run away to their reasons for feeling lonely—thereby revealing how we need to care for them. This book is a *must-read* for all parents. The way he identifies the children and creates individual action plans to ensure they get better emotionally, physically and psychologically before being reunited with their parents is indeed remarkable, along with the counselling provided to the parents of such children by him and his foundation.

In *Ten Great Escapes*, even though these children speak different languages and belong to various socio-economic backgrounds, Hariharan treats them equally, with dignity and respect. We often don't know how to treat our children—as parents or as a society. Once this problem is resolved, our country will progress in a constructive way. Each of these episodes teaches us how to improve our relationship with children, which is the only way to strengthen our upcoming generation. I sincerely wish Hariharan all the very best.

—Resul Pookutty
Oscar-winning Sound Engineer

Foreword

This is Hariharan's second book. In his first book *Runaway Children* published in 2015, he wrote about his harrowing experiences as a child who had run away from home three times. In his second book he continues with the theme of his first book and tells us ten stories about children who ran away from home.

Many philanthropists are working in charity organizations and doing social service. Each one tries to make a difference in their chosen area of activity. Many of them set apart a large part of their wealth for such activities.

Hariharan has chosen a very different area for social service. Children who are part of our lives disappear suddenly. Many parents go to police stations, newspaper offices and channels and other corridors of power trying desperately to get some information about their missing child. It is here that we must recognize the selfless service rendered by Hariharan. He has entered a domain into which not many people have ventured. Children who leave home for different reasons are left bewildered, not knowing where to go. Perhaps it is because he has gone through similar experiences that Hariharan has dedicated his life to helping such children.

His services in helping nearly 30,000 runaway children return to their homes deserve to be recorded in a separate chapter in a book that describes the history of social service. I have known him from the time I was a schoolboy and I know that he undertakes adventurous activities in a very unique way. The outcome would be far more interesting than anyone could have imagined. It is not surprising that Hariharan has chosen a field filled with challenges.

This book reveals the complexities of our times and offers guidance to anyone who dreams of a loving society.

My hearty good wishes to Shri Hariharan.

—Showkath Ali

Chairperson, Abu Dhabi Malayalee Samajam

Film Critic and Poet

Preface

There can be no keener revelation of a society's soul than the way in which it treats its children.

—Nelson Mandela

This book is the realization of a long-cherished desire. An incident that happened three years ago made me want to write this book. The day the police commissioner came to visit the children's home in Dongri. Children rescued from streets and railway stations are sent for rehabilitation to this centre. They stay there till their families come looking for them to take them back. If their parents are unable to travel, the children are then sent home with the help of the police. The commissioner had come to the centre to discuss, among other matters, the delay that occurred in reuniting children with their families due to the indifferent attitude of the police officers. After the meeting, he wished to meet the children. We went to the block where the girls were staying. The centre was sheltering nearly 300 boys and 70 girls. Our staff members had found more than 70 per cent of the boys here from railway stations. So I knew them well. The block that I was mostly affiliated with didn't have permission to shelter girls who came alone to the city, so I didn't know any of the girls here well.

The children were waiting in the hall. We went and sat with them and introduced ourselves. We spoke to them, mostly asking them about the facilities in the centre. We enquired whether they had any complaints or grievances. We noted down everything that they told us. We promised to find solutions to the problems.

When it was the turn of a child sitting in the fifth row, the response was that she had nothing to say. She had approached me several times before the meeting, requesting me to give her my phone as she wanted to call her mother who lived in Varanasi. Her mother said that her uncle was on his way to bring her back.

A little while later the superintendent told me that the girl's mother wanted to talk to me urgently. When I took the phone she seemed hesitant to talk. She asked me for my name and other details and said, 'I think I can trust you. I have no other way. I live with my parents. My husband left me. I work as a maid in the neighbouring houses. More than half of what I earn is spent on medicines for my father. We live in a slum, girls aren't safe here. It's difficult to educate her with the amount of money I make. Please don't send her back. I have no other way; please try to understand my situation. It isn't because I don't like her, I am helpless. Please don't tell her what I told you. She will be terribly upset if she knew that she can't come back; she is waiting for her uncle. Please find a way to keep her there. I can't think of anything other than this to keep her safe.'

I can't tell you how much her words shocked me. I wept holding the receiver. I couldn't bear to think of the helplessness of a mother who couldn't take her daughter home. How upset she must have been to talk to a stranger about her helplessness. My life has been dedicated to helping children. I know children who come from different circumstances. I understood their problems. But this mother's words shook me. Life at times shows us how powerless we are to help others.

That day returning from the centre I made a promise to myself. I would expand my activities and help as many children and their families as I could. There is a limit to what one can do alone, but with help we can do a lot. Even as we progress as a nation there are still many such families that live in dire need. Where do we begin our efforts to help them? What can we do to stop children from running away and leaving their families?

The most important thing is to try and understand children. No matter who you are—rich, poor, uneducated or high officials—you must know your children well. Give them the freedom to speak their mind. I am not talking only about children who run away from home. Do the children in our homes grow up in an atmosphere of love and happiness? Have we bothered to find out if they are happy? Just because they don't run away from their homes doesn't mean they are happy.

Children who are neglected by their parents, are physically or mentally tortured, have been sexually abused by their relatives or strangers or face difficulties while studying—all these are traumatic experiences for them. Can you imagine the effect these experiences can have on their minds? These wounds do not heal and can negatively affect their thoughts and beliefs.

Have you ever given thought to the way we bring up our children? Do we help them to evolve as responsible adults? Or do we inflict our dreams and ambitions on them? I am trying to create awareness about the above through this book.

At Samatol Foundation, we have rescued thousands of runaway children and sent them to their homes. I have included ten stories of such children in this book. They are true stories. You will get an idea of the different types of families from various strata of society. This book will also give you an idea about how children are influenced by their families and society.

These are not mere stories; they are a reminder. A reminder of the world that we need to create for children. Whether rich or poor, children are children. Their colour, the place they belong to or the language they speak makes no difference. They need our love and sympathy. They need our care.

Society should be able to help children overcome difficulties and motivate them to succeed in life. Families must encourage children to develop a positive outlook. They should ensure that the smiles on the faces of children never fade, and that their eyes shine bright with happiness. That is my aim in life. I have dedicated my life to helping them and set apart a large part of my money and time for the same. I want to see them live happily. Let me tell you the ways our foundation helps children. We rescue those who run away to Mumbai and help them. We try to trace their families and ensure that the children who go back home are happy and comfortable. Many children run away from the problems at home and some come to Mumbai hoping for a better life.

But the city is full of dangerous traps. Beneath the glitter and noise of Mumbai, there are marshlands, which suck you into their vortex.

Two members of our staff are always present at all railway stations in Mumbai.

The team consists of a man and a woman. They are trained to spot children who arrive alone or are abandoned and are in danger. The child may either be dressed shabbily and may be fatigued, or may be dressed as if going on a tour. It may be a boy doing odd jobs. They go up to any child who seems to be in an unsafe situation. When long-distance trains arrive on the platform, our team members are ready. They take positions at spots where they can see the passengers. One of them is on the platform and the other on the footbridge. They approach children who are alone with caution, and take care not to agitate them with questions. It is the female member of our team who first approaches the child. She gives them some water to drink and then the team members introduce themselves to the child by showing their identity cards and only then do they ask questions. They find out if the child is alone or is waiting for someone. If they find that the child is alone, they take precautions to not scare them. Usually someone from the Railway Protection Force is present. This helps us gain the confidence of the child.

The children we rescue from railway stations fall into three categories. In the first category are children who have run away from home for trivial reasons. More than 80 per cent of the children we rescue belong to this category. They may have been scolded by their father, performed badly in exams or quarrelled with a classmate. They cry when we ask them questions and tell us everything. They give us their parents' phone number and are ready to go home. Their faces reveal their love for their family and the relief that they can go home. It is easy to help them. We give their details to the nearest police station and send them to a children's home till their parents come to take them home. It is certain that their parents or guardian will arrive within a week.

In the second category are children who do not talk much and refuse to give us information about their families. We settle them in a temporary shelter. The important thing is to find out why they left home. Most often they would turn out to be victims of drug abuse, sexual abuse, child labour or human trafficking. When we see them first they are mostly in dirty clothes. We give them clean ones and have their hair cut after taking them to the shelter. They can rest, eat well and sleep. They can play with the other children there. After two or three days we start observing them. We try to find out what troubles them. Once their anxieties are allayed, they begin to talk to us openly. Then we try to locate their families and send them home safely. At times parents come to us after getting to know from the police that their child is with us. We make sure that the atmosphere at home is conducive for the child.

Then comes the third category—I belonged to this group. They are very strong and don't break under pressure. These are children who have suffered mental or physical abuse. It requires a concerted effort to help them recover. These children are taken to Swami Vivekananda Manparivartan Kendra, which functions under our foundation.

Manparivartan Kendra, what we call the ashram, is located on 30 acres of land in Mamnoli, Kalyan–Murbad Road. We have facilities there to rehabilitate children. Runaway children who need treatment that lasts for several months are taken there, where the atmosphere is that of a large family.

There are volunteers who take care of the children, hold them close and treat them like family members. Their love and affection help children forget their traumatic experiences. There are nearly 1,000 plants and trees on the campus. There are also 150 animals—cows, goats, dogs, cats, rabbits and tortoises. We have paddy cultivation on one acre of land. Is there a better way of teaching children the importance of agriculture?

The children have a set routine to follow—from 6 a.m. to 9 p.m. There are activities from yoga to tree climbing. Most classes are held under a huge tree. This helps the children relax and have fun. With nutritious food and exercise, the mental and physical health of the children improves. This programme lasts for three months. But within a month we see marked changes in the child's behaviour. Even the most introverted child starts talking about their troubles. They tell us everything about themselves including the reason they came to Mumbai.

The ashram has a team of experts including psychologists and counsellors. They speak to the children and encourage them. They also note down the specific characteristics of each child. This is analysed and a plan is prepared for each child to follow. This action plan helps children to overcome the dark memories of the past, fills their minds with positive thoughts and equips them to face the world with courage.

Almost 95 per cent of the children open up to us after 75 days of undergoing this course. We treat them in a very friendly manner. Even without us asking, they tell us about the problems that they faced at their homes. The next stage is to inform their families and help the child return home. We insist that children should grow up with their families, experiencing the love, warmth and security that only a family can give them. This is the main idea of our foundation. Along with rehabilitation of children we equally emphasize on reuniting the child with their family. We find another home if their parent's home is an unsafe place. We don't send children back if there is a high level of toxicity at home.

If the child is unsafe at home we make arrangements for the child to stay at the ashram and pursue their studies. At the ashram they can experience the warmth of a family and enjoy the companionship of their friends. If language is a problem we send the children to a hostel in their native place and they can go to a school there. Our volunteers keep in touch with them and we are informed about their welfare. A time is fixed for parents to visit them.

This is what we do.

I am not saying that you should stop whatever you are doing now and help runaway children. There is a simple way—adopt a child. I am not talking about legal adoption. Most of them don't need your money; they need your love and care. They want the confidence that you will be with them during ups and downs. If you think you can then pay their school and college fees. They need a guardian, a guide and a friend. Try to take on that role in the life of a child. You can make their lives happy. It's been three decades since I started to live for children. I have dedicated my life to finding runaway children and helping them to return home without them falling into danger. Each child, each family is a story, a lesson. I am learning the intricacies of these lives.

At times it requires months of efforts to send a child back to their home. But the reunion gives us happiness that cannot be described. It has to be experienced. It is our greatest reward.

Parents and guardians arrive at the ashram almost every day to take their children home. Yet we organize a function for these reunions thrice a year. We invite police officers, judges or ministers as special guests for these functions. Parents who have spent months desperately searching for their missing children are finally reunited with them in front of a large audience.

It is an emotional moment. When parents get their children back they realize the importance of a family and relationships. They take care to ensure that there is no reason for their child to leave home again. No child wishes to leave home; we adults push them out. Not allowing them to live peacefully and happily we compel them out into the streets on strange paths. We are responsible for the dangers children face when they leave home. This is something we say repeatedly. We say the same thing at any event in the presence of distinguished guests and the families of these children. No one can disagree with this. The stars at this function are our children. They talk about their experiences; they sing and dance. They are not the children who left home in pain. They are confident and ready to face the challenges of the world and they have a clear idea about their future. When the families get the children back they hug them; they laugh and cry. The children hold their parents' hands tightly. I sit in a corner watching all this, watching the brilliant colours of life unfolding before me.

I can feel my eyes brimming with tears. We have been organizing these reunions for years now. But I cry each time. I can't stop crying when I see children run across the stage towards their parents.

I know the joy they experience because I have been through this myself. A runaway child—not once but thrice. My experiences taught me how society treats runaway children. Life in the streets makes you a different person. I realized my destiny during the days I lived on the streets of Mumbai. A child's life is not to be spent on a street. And that is why it is my karma to send children who run away from home back to their families.

That is the mantra of my life—my destiny.

I told you that an incident that happened three years ago pushed me to write this book. But there is someone who kept telling me to publish a book containing stories of some children—my close friend who works in the world of cinema—Resul Pookutty. His suggestions helped me select the 10 stories for this book. Thanking Resul, I humbly invite you to the world of these stories.

The Musician

It happened three years ago. It was past midnight when the incessant ringing of my phone woke me up. Half asleep I stared at the screen; it was my Malayali friend Bhaskar. He was not someone who rang me during odd hours at night. I answered his call. He was at the police station and something gruesome had happened. A child had been brutally raped by his own friends. Hearing the news Bhaskar had rushed to the police station, but the police were refusing to record the FIR and were not taking the child to the hospital. They were waiting for the child's parents to arrive. The child was bleeding profusely. Bhaskar was afraid he would bleed to death. He had called me as he knew that I am a member of the child welfare committee.

I immediately rang up some high officials in the police force and they got in touch with the concerned officers. It was then that Bhaskar called me again. The child's parents had arrived at the police station. They took the child home refusing to file a complaint. Bhaskar pleaded with them to register a complaint but they paid no heed.

I have seen many sensitive cases become complicated due to red-tapism and that is why I used all my influence to get the case registered that night itself. But I was filled with anger at the way the child's parents behaved. They were worried about the humiliation they would have to face if the news about the rape got around. I don't understand how people could think in this manner. Shouldn't the parents have been compassionate towards their son? Their decision was instead helping the criminals. Why can't our society accept the fact that boys too can be victims of rape? A hundred questions rose to my mind.

Bhaskar too was confused. He asked the police officers if there was any possibility of filing a case. But the police officers were helpless as they couldn't take action without a complaint.

He was raped on the night of his birthday just as the celebrations were ending. The police put forward an absurd argument—as the boy had turned 18 that night, they couldn't file a child sexual abuse case against the offenders. Bhaskar reiterated that the child needed urgent medical attention. I too was worried about his condition. Bhaskar went to the child's home. He had to plead with the parents for nearly two hours before they agreed to take the child to the hospital. Bhaskar later told me that even as he was requesting them to take the child to the hospital, his parents were blaming and cursing him for having brought humiliation upon the family.

I was using all my resources to get the police to the spot where the crime had occurred. As the FIR had not been filed, the hospitals refused to admit the child. Finally his father agreed to file a complaint. After wasting several hours at the police station and the hospital, by the time he was admitted, he was on the verge of losing consciousness.

The next morning I went to the hospital. Bhaskar was waiting for me at the gate. He took me to the ward. It was a psychiatry ward—bustling with people—as there were no beds available elsewhere. Bhaskar whispered in my ear that his name was Jithin. I was heartbroken to see him. I still cannot forget the sight. A tall, well-built boy was cowering in a corner of the hospital bed, weeping. He had covered his face with a bed sheet and was trembling. There was no one with him. In the bed next to him was a psychiatric patient covered in blood, shouting and rolling around. He had been tied to the cot. How can I ever forget that scene?

For a moment I did not know what to do, but I said to him, 'Don't worry son. We will get you discharged by evening.'

Very slowly I prepared Jithin for the medical

examination. He kept a tight hold on my hand. Trembling in fear and weeping copiously he went through the medical examination. I held him tight and kept talking to him. In the course of our conversation I understood that he liked McDonald's burgers. He also told me who his favourite Hollywood star was. A friend of mine contacted the actor while my driver brought a burger from McDonald's.

It was when I handed him the burger that he looked at me for the first time. He stopped crying and I knew that he was slowly coming out of shock. I felt like crying then and my eyes brimmed with tears. His favourite movie star spoke to him over a video call and Jithin couldn't believe it. He smiled. I still do not know how to thank the great actor who had taken time out to talk to him. It seemed as though Jithin had forgotten the hospital and the painful experience that had brought him there. The distraction was like a treatment and he became calmer.

I knew that he had to be shifted from the noisy ward. As the medical examination was concluded and he had been given first aid I asked the doctor whether he could be discharged, to which the doctor agreed. But the formalities took so long that he had to spend the night in the psychiatry ward. At midnight the patient in the bed next to his turned violent. The man who had been tied to the bed escaped and tried to attack Jithin. The poor boy had to bear the brunt of two attacks.

When I enquired the next morning I was told that his parents had taken Jithin home. I didn't receive any other details. I wanted him to go for counselling. My years of experience in dealing with such cases had taught me that unless Jithin's mental health was taken care of, he would lose his self-confidence and his behaviour would change. Though Bhaskar continued to enquire about Jithin, his parents refused to divulge any information about him.

After a whole day had passed, Jithin's parents told Bhaskar that they had locked him up in a room. Bhaskar requested them to take Jithin for counselling but they refused. He even told them to at least be kind to him, but Jithin's parents were only concerned about their reputation and tried to defend their stand by spouting philosophy and logic. They were like teachers caning a student in order to teach him a lesson. His mother decided that all this had happened because Jithin had fallen into bad company and the best thing to do was to lock him up.

Jithin's family was not well off and they managed to make ends meet with difficulty. Jithin loved his mother. He had been a good guitarist from childhood. He used to compose songs and participate in music programmes. His mother never hesitated to use the money Jithin earned from those programmes. Bhaskar had first met

Jithin at a music programme and recognizing his talent had befriended him. Bhaskar knew that Jithin's heart was full of love and he was emotionally fragile. Bhaskar and I decided to wait for two days before meeting Jithin's parents again to convince them to take him for counselling.

But unable to bear his parents' anger, Jithin attempted to commit suicide and this worsened the situation at his home. They blamed him for humiliating them. We rushed to his house and I spoke to his mother at length. Luckily, she listened to us. We took him to a doctor and slowly he began to recover.

We should also know how Jithin got into a situation that caused him so much harm. He lived in a tiny village on the Maharashtra–Gujarat border. His family did not take good care of him. They never bothered to find out what he wanted or what his interests were. When he won a prize or did well in an exam, no one bothered to hold him close and congratulate him. The whole family was focused on getting Jithin's elder sister married; no one had time for him.

When he realized that he had to take care of himself, he created a world of his own. Life was moving on with his studies and playing games with a few friends when his sister was married. He used to go to Mumbai often to visit his sister and he decided to join a college there. It was then that the lockdown was declared and everything went awry. He was stuck in his sister's house. Though his father repeatedly told him to go back and continue his studies in the village, Jithin didn't want to leave Mumbai. He was alone in the city and did not have enough money to join an online course. He felt neglected in his sister's house and his only solace was his mobile phone. It created a wonderland for him—new friends and a new world. Slowly his life became colourful. The virtual world became more real and meaningful than the actual world. He discussed his doubts and secrets with his friends on Facebook. He spent hours with them. The innocent 17-year-old felt loved and wanted for the first time in his life.

He met Dev and Salim online. They were the same age as him and belonged to his village (that is what they told him). They became close quite quickly. Jithin told them about his family and his dreams. He had never discussed all this with his mother or sister. Slowly they started discussing girlfriends. Dev shared a picture of a beautiful girl saying she was his girlfriend. Salim too followed suit by sharing another picture of a pretty girl, supposedly his girlfriend. Jithin did not have a girlfriend nor did he desire to have one (though Jithin had many girls as his friends, they did not have a romantic relationship). Though he tried telling them that he did not have a girlfriend they kept urging him to get one. Finally, Jithin requested one of his female friends to send him her picture so he could share it claiming she was his girlfriend, and she sent him her photograph.

As the lockdown restrictions were being lifted one by one, the demands of his virtual friends began changing. When hotels and restaurants reopened, these friends decided to meet at a restaurant along with their girlfriends. Salim and Dev made plans. It was Jithin's birthday. The three of them decided to meet at a nearby place and then go to a restaurant in Salim's car. They planned to meet at six' o clock in the evening as Jithin's 'girlfriend' had to get home early. When Jithin and his friend reached the location, they saw Salim and his gang. Neither Dev nor their girlfriends were there. As she felt uncomfortable, Jithin's friend left immediately. What awaited Jithin was terrible. He was cruelly raped. They stole his purse and he was nearly dead when they dumped him in an isolated place.

I met Jithin and spoke with him over the phone when he was undergoing counselling. He couldn't face his family, his mother or his younger sister. The feeling of having been cheated gnawed at him.

I have met many sexually abused children who drown in sorrow, whose faces are shadowed with the trauma they suffered, who have lost the will to live. They withdraw into themselves fearing the world that has hurt them. It is heartbreaking to watch them sever ties with their family and friends one by one, the colour draining from their lives, allowing themselves to become listless, slowly breaking away from the buds of life. It is an arduous and time-consuming task to bring them back to the mainstream by freeing them from the chains of fear and guilt. But when I hold them close I experience the presence of God, of divinity.

'First stop blaming yourself, it is not your fault, my son. What has happened has happened, put it behind you and move on. You cannot define your life by one bad incident. You have your dreams and ambitions.' I spoke to him for a long time and then I took him to the ashram one day.

It was then that I realized just how smart Jithin was. He was very talented and his thinking was clear. There were a few children at the ashram who had been sexually abused. Some children had run away from home unable to bear the violence or neglect, children who had run away from life to the great metropolis of Mumbai. Some children had come to the ashram seeking love and compassion. In the midst of other children Jithin was happy and excited. They kept talking about school and the games they played. He went around the ashram with them and enquired about the activities of the Foundation that helped runaway children. He was slowly gaining the ability to overcome the horrifying experience. He visited the ashram many times and spoke to the children there and played with them. We felt that he liked the ashram. I asked one of the children, 'When Jithin comes here what do you talk about? Cinema or school?' He looked at me in surprise. 'Don't you know? Jithin is a great musician. We were talking about which songs to dance to for the online music competition.' I had never thought of him as a musician. He was interested in choreography also. He filled me with amazement, he was a talented singer and a guitarist.

Slowly Jithin returned to his normal life. He started engaging in many activities and remaining positive at all times. I had managed to get him admission to a college in Mumbai. Just as we were hoping that he would put the past behind him when classes began, Jithin disappeared.

He went missing from his sister's house in the city. He did not go to his home in the village nor did he get in touch with his friends. It was as if he wanted to escape from everyone he knew.

Some memories burn like embers and they burst into flames brushing the ashes aside. I was pained that I had not perceived the pain he hid beneath his smiles. He might not have been able to bear the humiliation that his ego suffered. How did I ever think that he had returned to his regular life happily? I realized that he needed not just solace but a reason to live. He must emerge a victor. We were trying for this. I felt very guilty.

We prayed that he would be safe and that he would not try to take his life. After many days he called his friends—he wanted money. We acted promptly. All his friends requested him to come back. We were able to convince him that we loved him and were arranging for everything he needed. Luckily he came back. Anything could have happened to him. Children who suffer from sexual abuse usually follow a behavioural pattern of running away. It was sheer luck that we got him back. Chances had been high of him either committing suicide or never coming back to us.

All this began with an online chat session. Parents always warn children against speaking with strangers but they rarely know what their children are up to in the virtual world. When will we tell our children about the dangers that lurk in the virtual world? Where do we go wrong?

Jithin went through many counselling sessions and began staying at the ashram. It took several months for him to recover. All of us kept talking to him. We urged him to forget the past and focus on the future. He did succeed in putting the past behind him.

Though he went back home, he was a frequent visitor at the ashram. The children surrounded him when he came. They asked him to choreograph the dance for the music competition. I noticed that he was a completely changed person when he was immersed in music. Soon he began to perform for music shows. He was filled with energy, his eyes brimming with confidence.

We had spoken to his parents in great detail. 'Children his age may not be at home all the time, but we must ensure that there is a place for them to come back to. That should be a home to him. This is the responsibility of parents. Children deserve love and a feeling of security.'

Though late, they had realized their mistake and were willing to make amends. During the counselling sessions they attended, Jithin's parents realized how much their fears and insecurities had affected their children. We were convinced that he would no longer be neglected at home.

Today, Jithin is a well-known rock star, not only in Mumbai but all over India. The band that he leads is quite famous. In the rhythm of his music and in each movement on the stage he searches for his self. Amidst the awards and applause heaped on him, he realizes that his greatest triumph was his ability to rise like a phoenix. He spends his free time trying to hone the talents of the children of the ashram. When I understood Jithin's philosophy that conceptualizes music as a spiritual space that heals, I too realized that music is a balm that heals wounds. Jithin is on his way to becoming a world-famous star.

The Kleptomaniac

'I began stealing when I was five years old. I stole a sweet from a nearby shop. I felt happy when I stole it. I can still feel the crunchiness of the plastic wrapping paper in my hand. I laughed a lot that day. It was as if I had defeated everyone and won a game on my own. I felt as though I had won a marathon or kicked a ball higher than anyone else. For me it was a treasure that I had found and managed to hide from my family and friends.

'Even when I turned 10, I did not stop stealing. It gave me great pleasure. If you ask me why I stole, I do not have an answer. I used to steal inexpensive things—a toy, a book or a sweet. Though many of the things that I stole were of no value to me, I felt great pleasure in stealing. Sweets and toys did not interest me, yet I continued to steal these things. I often stole used pencils and packs of playing cards.

'I did not have many friends in my early teens. I was often lonely and bored and then the urge to steal a sweet or a matchbox or a ball from a house nearby would rise within me, it was a hunger I couldn't control. When I stole something I felt as satiated as if I had eaten a feast. No one ever knew that I was stealing. My friends and neighbours may have suspected, but no one ever caught me red-handed. But I was fed up with life at home. Shahpur was not very far from Mumbai, and I had nothing to do here. Even if I left home no one would be upset. My mother died when I was a child. My father would get drunk every day. I only had my grandmother to talk to. When my grandmother passed away it was just my father and I at home. We wouldn't see each other for days on end. I have never seen my father ever concerned about where I was.

'One day I boarded a train for Mumbai. I had never been there before, but I had often fantasized about working in a bustling city.'

This is what Babu told our group of workers when they saw him at the railway station. He seemed unperturbed when he spoke to them.

A young James Bond! That is what I thought when I first met Babu. When our staff saw Babu at the railway station, he was alone, but he did not seem anxious or nervous. It was as if he had a place to stay and there was either someone waiting for him or there was some plan in place for him. As our team had seen many children like Babu who look unflustered despite being alone in a strange city, they knew that these children hid their fear beneath the façade of confidence. It would take only a few hours before the mask slipped and they began behaving like children. When our team spoke to Babu he behaved as though he had been waiting for them. They did not need to persuade him at all.

After the official formalities, Babu came to our Swami Vivekananda Manparivartan Kendra.

As he knew Hindi and Marathi it was easy to communicate with him. It was as though he had got on the train to come to the ashram. He was very talkative and easily befriended the children in the ashram. He got on well with the staff as well. Though he discussed almost everything, he never spoke about his home. He just gave us a vague picture of the family that he had left behind. This was a story quite similar to what many of the children we rescue from the streets tell us—they have lost their parents, or their grandmother can't look after them, or they have come in search of a job so that they can take care of their grandmother. What made Babu different was that he told us about his penchant for stealing. He did not tire of the ashram, he became friends with everyone. I once found him in the kitchen helping the cook, on another day he was in the garden telling the children how to plant a seedling. The children of the ashram thought that he was a hero as he could do anything. He could climb trees and swing from its branches, he would walk on the edge of the wall and jump down. He was a swift runner as well. Our counsellors spent a lot of time with him. They put him down as a pleasant boy with a positive attitude. He loved all the children of the ashram, he never blamed anyone if something went wrong, he enthusiastically participated in all activities of the ashram and was the first to offer to take up new responsibilities.

As we did not have any information about his family we decided to keep him in the ashram till he completed the prescribed three months of study. He was thrilled to be included in this programme and was quite eager to learn new things. But the ashram began to experience certain unprecedented events. Many things started vanishing from the ashram. Small things, such as pens from the library, a box of sweets from the storeroom and cheese cubes that the cook had kept safe, started disappearing each day. The workers doubted whether some of the glass figurines in the curio cupboard had walked away. As we had an effective surveillance system and our team had a good rapport with the children, we quickly discovered the culprit. We knew that Babu had not done it intentionally. The counsellors had told us that he was a kleptomaniac. They watched him very closely.

They saw how he looked at something on a table or in a cupboard. They noted the dexterity with which he threw the thing he was stealing into his pocket or inside his shirt or into the cuffs of his shirt sleeve. During this time he would be completely focused on what he was doing. It was as if he was involved in some serious activity. When we continued to watch him we realized that he was not planning to steal but he was doing so inadvertently. It was always unexpected; the urge to steal whatever was in sight would control him. Medical science considers kleptomania as a mental aberration. Kleptomania is the inability to resist the urge to steal items and the loss of control over this urge. People with kleptomania don't compulsively steal for personal gain; they do not plan to steal—it is an uncontrollable urge for self-satisfaction. It is a sudden decision. They may not steal expensive things; it could be a pencil, a tube of cream or a small piece of jewellery. Most often they do not even use the things they steal. They may either discard what they have stolen or give it to someone else. Sometimes they keep it back in the place from where they took it. Usually, kleptomaniacs keep stealing when they feel that they won't get caught; they do not actually realize the repercussions of what will happen if they are caught stealing. Kleptomaniacs wage a constant war with their emotions and self-control. An experienced medical practitioner needs to assess the situation and structure a treatment plan very objectively, scientifically and without any preconceived notions. It is said that at times medication may be required. When we understood what Babu's problem was we knew that he required medical attention. Our team of counsellors started the treatment. They assessed the dangers that could be caused by his behaviour and spoke to Babu at length.

This is how they reported the case—Babu knew what he was doing, he was in fact proud of it. He had no difficulty in admitting that he stole things. But why did he steal? 'It gives me a sense of power. I feel I am smart. Even when shops have security systems I can steal without getting caught. As I can steal very easily, I keep wanting to try and do it.' They recorded his response.

The next step was to make him understand that what he was doing was a crime and that the law could punish him by sending him to a juvenile home. That what begins as a trivial misdeed can lead to grave offences, even developing into an urge to steal expensive things from large stores that have effective surveillance systems. We began the herculean task of treating Babu; we tried to involve him in discussions to convince him that kleptomania was like drug addiction. It was then that Babu began to think about this habit that he had had from a very young age.

'I never plan to steal. Even when I am sitting in a friend's house I feel the urge to steal. After stealing I feel that I have accomplished something and that it will remain undetected. This fills me with joy,' he told us during our discussions.

He had no pleasant memories of his home or his childhood. The act of stealing was the only thing that gave him some validation for his existence.

We told him, 'But what you do has serious consequences. After a while you will start feeling guilty and this will have a negative impact on your mental health. You may also end up committing a serious crime.'

He listened to what we were telling him. He resolved to stop stealing. He said that he would stop taking things when he desired pleasure. We decided to give him three months to come to terms with his new life. He fell into the rhythm of life at the ashram. We saw that he was happy when he interacted with other children. We watched him constantly and felt that he had succeeded in overcoming his kleptomania. No one reported that they had lost anything. We felt that Babu was preparing to resume his studies. But one day he disappeared. We were shocked because the ashram had a very efficient surveillance system. It is not easy to deal with children who run away from home so we were always vigilant. But Babu proved us wrong.

We searched for him and also checked to find out where our security system had failed (and we soon set it right).

Our counsellor said, 'Maybe he did not like being controlled by you and he wanted to live on his own terms.' It is not easy to categorize children like Babu who crave adventure. They are always seeking something new. I had seen children like him before. Once you instil in them the value of good education, it is easy for them to pursue their studies and take the right path.

I felt that Babu would come back once the thrill of living alone faded and he became conscious of the dangers of living in the streets. We wondered whether he would continue to stay in Mumbai or go home to his village. We were upset that we couldn't help him. We hoped he would return, but three months passed without Babu coming back to the ashram. Then one day one of our staff saw him at another railway station. He looked as happy as he had been before. He looked as calm as James Bond had after a hair-raising adventure. It was a relief that we found him in safe surroundings and that we were able to bring him back. When I saw him, I immediately asked, 'What happened? Why did you run away? You had the freedom to speak to me or anyone else here.'

He looked at me vacantly. I felt he had aged a lot in

those three months. He did not look like a 14-year-old boy, it seemed as if he was in his late twenties. But he still looked happy.

After a while he said, 'I was bored here.'

'Were you bored by your studies or by the way of life in the ashram?'

'I can't live like this. I know that all of you are good people and that you want the best for me. But I can't continue to stay here, I need excitement and that is why I ran away.'

For several days our team spoke to him for long hours. We tried to convince him to view his life from a different perspective and told him of the dangers of living a life filled with uncertainties. We told him that instead of becoming a criminal he had several opportunities to get a job and live in Mumbai like he had always dreamt of.

Babu took some time to ponder over what we told him. We did not disturb him during this time. Finally he came to us and said, 'I will live here like the other children, but you must allow me to go out for a whole day every month. I promise to return within 24 hours. On that day I will do what I want. I will never get into trouble and I promise not to drag you into any problems.'

It was a strange condition that he had put forward to us. No other child had requested something like this, but Babu was different.

We discussed his demand and we decided to let him go out for a day and to watch him without him knowing. On his day out he would either go to the beach or a shopping centre. He would eat at various roadside eateries and come back to the ashram the next day. In the first few months he would bring back money or pencils or sweets and distribute them among the children of the ashram as if he were an elder brother who had come home for a vacation. We did not ask him anything about that.

After a few months things changed. Babu still brought treats for the children but it was with the money that we gave him. He never stole after that. No matter how great the temptation was he never took anything that wasn't his. He was able to curb the urge to steal. He had cured himself. With the help of the police and the local NGOs we were able to locate Babu's father. We got permission from him to allow Babu to stay in the ashram and continue his studies. We felt that he was happy to know Babu was safe, though he had not even realized that his son had left home. Some homes are strange—the lack of love and affection leads some parents to forget about their children.

Babu passed class 10th with good grades. He is now in class 12th. No one has complained about his behaviour, neither his school nor the people he interacts with. He has changed. He has no complaints about anyone; he is mindful of his surroundings and tries to find his own happiness. We respect him for that.

The Runaways

It was nearly midnight. Ravi felt a bit scared. Samanth had told him not to worry as he had planned everything right from getting to the railway station from home to the time they would reach Mumbai. Ravi wished he was as bold as Samanth. Both of them were 13 years old, but Samanth knew a lot more than Ravi did. In fact this trip was his idea.

Samanth would often tell Ravi, 'Shall we go somewhere?' He usually asked this question when he saw Ravi in a despondent state. When Ravi did badly in his exams he would be silent on the way home. He wouldn't laugh at Samanth's jokes and walk with his head hung low. Though Samnath would ask Ravi what the matter was, he knew well what awaited Ravi at home.

It was not just his parents who would ask him about his marks, there would be a crowd waiting for him. He lived in a joint family with his uncles and aunts. Like Ravi said, 'There are many people at home who wait to tear me apart, but there is not a single person to comfort me.'

In his last exam, he only got 12 marks out of 50 in mathematics. When he got back home he felt as if he had been arrested by the police. 'You will fail in class 7. No one here has done so badly in maths.' The accusations struck him like arrows. It was not just when he did badly in exams that Ravi felt helpless. He would be scolded for playing and they would ask him to study. If he sat down with his favourite *Hardy Boys* book, someone would say, 'Why can't you go out and play like other children? Why are you wasting your time reading stories?'

Ravi often felt that he was living in a circus tent. A place filled with people, a constant stream of visitors and an army of servants. Everyone had an opinion about the other person's life and they would voice it loudly. The children were treated like circus animals, brought out into the ring and whipped into obedience. The older children were just as bad. The school toppers among them were the worst. They would knock him on his head and call him stupid. They would rag him, asking whether he would pass, but when he asked for their help in his studies, they would shoo him away and say that he was an idiot.

Ravi always wondered why he was the only child who was targeted though there were many children at home. He did not know why his parents didn't protect him and told others to leave him alone. He was constantly besieged by these questions that rose in his mind. He hardly ever saw his busy father. He knew that he was a high official in Tripura. Everyone spoke about his father's position. He worked with ministers. He came home very late and rarely spoke to his son. He had a couple of stock questions to ask Ravi, 'How are your studies? What are your future plans?' He often wished that his father would speak of something else. He wondered if his father knew who his friends were, what games they played and what they spoke about. Why did he go on asking about his future plans when he did not know anything about his son's present? His mother was always busy. He thought to himself, 'Does anyone really care about me?'

None of the movies that he watched had homes like his, he thought. In the movies families were happy and people liked each other. He had only seen families that joked, sang songs and ate together in the movies he watched. He believed that relatives who teased and hurt each other's feelings existed only in his family.

The Diwali vacations were drawing near. Everyone was preparing for the festivities. The number of visitors would increase. Ravi wasn't interested in all this. He was worried that he would have to face his relatives and the constant stream of visitors all the time. All he wanted to do was retreat into a corner with a book.

He didn't want to talk to anyone, he felt weary of it all. He felt that someone would upset him with their words at any time.

He tried to talk to his mother about this, but his mother as usual paid no attention. She did not realize that her son was slipping into depression. She told him to stop acting crazy. Ravi knew that he wasn't pretending. He had lost all interest in going to school and in his studies. But even then his mother did not understand his plight. Slowly he felt that Samanth was the only person he could depend on.

One day he mustered the courage to tell his mother that he wasn't interested in going to school, but that unleashed a storm. All his relatives scolded him. 'Arrogant, lazy, disobedient' epithets were showered on him. When his mother slapped him his home became a dangerous place for him. Thinking of the other after-effects that would follow his announcement of wanting to quit his studies, he sank into despair.

Samanth knew the situation when he asked Ravi, 'Shall we go to Mumbai?' Ravi did not think twice before agreeing.

Ravi wanted to leave home. He hoped that at least his absence would help his mother understand what he was going through. He felt that silence was the best reply that he could give his relatives who had mocked him. It only required some courage to take that step. He didn't know what he would do in Mumbai. Samanth told him that they would go sightseeing in Mumbai—see the Gateway of India, walk down Marine Drive and go to the beach as Tripura did not have one. He had seen beaches only in movies. Though he had travelled he had not been to a beach. He longed to go to a beach and touch the waves. He wanted to eat at wayside eateries. When Samanth spoke of eating panipuri and bhelpuri, Ravi felt the dark clouds of depression lifting. When Samanth said that they may get to see Shah Rukh Khan, Ravi knew that he had to go to Mumbai. But he was scared. Where would they live in Mumbai? He knew that it wasn't a small city like Agartala. He comforted himself with the thought that he had quite a large amount of money with him. He had saved all the money he had received as gifts for Diwali. He asked Samanth whether the money would suffice. Samanth told him that they would work when they ran out of money. That was Mumbai—children could earn money by working.

Samanth was of the opinion that when they had no money left, they would come back home. Then no one would trouble them. They could think of it as a huge adventure. Ravi felt that Samanth knew everything. He had met Samanth two years ago when they were in class 5. He was the same even then—he didn't care about anyone or anything. He was always up to something. He would skip school often and wander around. He wasn't bothered about being scolded. He told Ravi that he was tired of his home and school. Ravi decided to leave home only because he trusted Samanth and looked up to him. Ravi confided in Samanth and told him of the troubles he faced at home and school. Samanth had a solution to all problems, like this idea of going to Mumbai. He planned everything right from the ticketless travel from Agartala to Mumbai. Ravi felt that this trip would be a lot of fun.

Ravi was able to prepare for the journey quite easily. As Diwali had ended everyone was busy. He packed a bag with two sets of clothes, a *Hardy Boys* novel and a Rubik's cube. He filled the bag with Diwali sweets and a few oranges. He put his purse inside a book. Putting his bag beneath his study table he went to bed. He knew that he wouldn't be able to sleep. He had to get out before midnight after which the gate would be locked. Samanth would be waiting for him. Their train was at 5 a.m.

Why do children run away? Most of us would say that it is because of poverty or violence at home. Most of us are still under the misconception that only children who are from marginalized communities or live in poverty run away from home. Ravi's story challenges this notion. A child from a prosperous family, a child who lived in comfort decided to run away. His home was his problem. Children are always like that. All their anxieties, problems and worries are centred on their homes. It is the atmosphere at home that makes them brave and gives them the confidence to face the world. But most often it is home that pushes them out. They reach a point where they feel that the insecurities of a strange place are better than the life they lead at home.

Ravi was not different. He belonged to a well-known family in Agartala. He lived in a big house, his father was a high official and his relatives were all highly placed. He could have done anything he wanted; yet at the age of 13 he chose to run away from home.

We cannot choose our family, but we can choose our friends. Samanth was Ravi's source of confidence. It was only because of Samanth that Ravi decided to go to Mumbai. He got the love and affection he craved from home from his friend. The first thing that struck me when I saw them was that they were both very smart. Our staff too said that it was a wonderful performance they put up at the railway station. When our team saw the two boys at Chhatrapati Shivaji Terminus, they tried to protect them from getting lost by holding them close. But the boys weren't nervous or anxious at all. Though their Hindi was not fluent, they spoke with confidence and said that they knew their way around Mumbai. They did not even listen to our staff.

'We aren't coming with you. We don't need to meet anyone. We don't have any problems. What is your problem?'

Ravi's body language seemed to suggest that he was not an ordinary child. He was trying to imitate his elders and act as if he was 'cool'. Samanth looked even more confident than Ravi did.

Even our team with their years of experience in dealing with hundreds of children were surprised by the confidence of these children. No matter how bold they seemed, usually children would become bewildered by the chaos at the station teeming with people and would start to regret their decision of running away. But Ravi was very confident, perhaps because Samanth was with him. When our team insisted that the children should come away with them, Ravi, putting on the tone of a movie star, said, 'Do you know who my father is?'

Samanth immediately added, 'His father is a big shot. If they knew about this, the police would come and arrest you for blocking our way. We have come to Mumbai for sightseeing. We will go back only after that.' Saying that they roamed around the railway station behaving like the hero and his sidekick in the movies.

The staff caught up with them and without asking

Ravi who his father was, they began to talk to them. They asked the boys where they would stay in Mumbai. The team told them that the hotels wouldn't rent rooms to children. The police would be alerted. They may file a case against them. They also told them about the danger of being kidnapped by underworld dons. Their limbs would be chopped off and they would be used for begging. The team spoke to them about the other dangers that lurked in the city. But several hours passed before the boys agreed to leave the railway station with the team.

They found it easier to convince Samanth. Though the idea of running away had been his, he was a bit scared. Seeing Samanth waver, Ravi too decided to accompany our staff. The team brought them to the centre after completing all the formalities. When I met them they were behaving quite differently from the way they had at the railway station. Ravi was silent, Samanth did all the talking. He did not tell us anything about their families though. We too decided not to probe. Most children are quite unwilling to talk about their families and some of them lie.

Ravi and Samanth were always together. They ate together and walked around the ashram together. They kept a distance from other children and spoke only when they were asked questions, even though most of the children at the ashram were around their age. They did not join even when the children played football or cricket. We did not force them to do anything.

It was easy to guess that Ravi and Samanth came from rich families. They wore branded clothes. Ravi's watch and shoes were expensive. The game that Samanth had with him was not like the ones children usually played with. Two days passed. When Ravi saw that no one was pressurizing him or plaguing him with questions, his behaviour changed. He responded to the affection shown to him.

'We were wrong to run away. People at home will be worried about us,' Ravi told Samanth. He had been brooding about this for the past two days. When he had boarded the train it had seemed like a great adventure. They could wander around, look at the sights and have fun without being bothered. But after reaching the ashram, he felt guilty. He felt that he had made a mistake.

Samanth too was troubled by the thought of home. Only his mother and elder brother were at home. His father worked in Delhi and came home only once a month. No one scolded him, but he did not like being at home. He was always in search of an adventure.

The boys thought about what they would do next. 'Don't think too much. We are happy here, aren't we? The people here are nice to us. Let us stay here for a while. This is also an adventure,' Samanth told Ravi. As he was used to agreeing with whatever Samanth said Ravi too decided to stay on. They slowly started to interact with the staff and other children. The staff always gave the children a lot of freedom. When Ravi realized that they were listening to him without ever blaming him, he started to open up.

'I should not have run away from home.' This was the first thing that Ravi told us.

'We had no other way, that's why we ran away,' Samanth added.

We realized that the children had decided to open up to us after days of silence. We knew that they were speaking to us after having discussed what to say. They never spoke about their families and we did not press them for information as we knew it would take time for them to trust us. Even when children decide to talk, they don't give out all the information at once, it takes time. It is futile to force them to talk.

We spoke to them at length and were able to convince them that they could set things right. The most important thing was to instil confidence in them. Then their thoughts would become positive and they would be able to see life clearly. Everyone in the ashram was willing to support them.

Once they started talking to us, things changed

dramatically. Ravi became a hero for the children there. They would go to him for help. Most of the children at the ashram attended school but some of them studied in the ashram itself. Ravi helped them in their studies. They gathered around him when he explained maths, science and English lessons to them. He never tired of teaching them. Though he was only in class 7 he knew quite a lot. Maybe it was because he went to a good school or perhaps because of the influence of his family. He not only spoke English fluently but also taught the children well. He explained grammar and gave them tips to improve their spoken English.

Akshay was the youngest member of the ashram then. He was 10 years old. We had rescued him from the streets a few months ago. No one had come to take him home. His face revealed his sorrow. He was quite good at studies and very friendly. He became very close to Samanth and Ravi. The three of them were always together. Akshay showed them around the farm and the garden and introduced them to the children and the workers. In the evenings everyone got together and chatted.

Ravi lost his supercilious attitude. When he had first come to the ashram his body language clearly showed that he felt it was beneath his dignity to stay at the ashram. He did not even like to reply to questions. He changed within a few days and started mingling with everyone. He liked to help the children with their studies, he would even tell them about the books he had read. We had never seen such a young child who taught maths and science so well. He was a natural. He succeeded in winning the children over in no time. He tried to improve the way they behaved. He liked to show them how to wash their hands properly. He taught them table manners and the importance of not wasting food.

He had never been given so much love before. No one had given him any importance. He had never experienced the love of a family at his home. Life in the ashram was very different and he wanted to make the most of each moment he spent there. Samanth too was eager to help the children with their studies. They did not want to think about home or going back.

We too felt quite positive about the boys. As they had told us, they were not ordinary children. But we still didn't know why they had left home.

It had been a month since Ravi and Samanth had come to the ashram. Ravi's teaching had improved and he was always eager to try something new. He did not hesitate to work in the garden or kitchen or to bathe the cows. He worked with enthusiasm.

We did not receive any information about their families. I spoke to Samanth alone but he did not divulge any information. Samanth told us a story we were familiar with. He said that their parents weren't alive and that they had come to Mumbai to find work so that they could help their grandmothers.

'If that is so then why did you act so pricey at the railway station?'

We just tried to fool you. We have seen such things in movies, we thought that you would leave us alone.'

Though they spoke to us, we knew very little about them except that they were from Tripura.

Children who run away from their homes suffer from mental tension and our psychologists help them deal with this. These conversations help to dispel their anxieties. Though they spoke to Ravi and Samanth, they did not get any information. So we decided to give it time. Once they became calm and started trusting us more, they would give us all the information. It may take a month or two but children cannot hold on for longer than that. They would start talking to us. We were sure that the two boys would definitely tell us about themselves.

Ravi and Samanth opened up to the counsellors.

'We thought for a long time whether we should tell you about us. But how can we keep a secret from people who have treated us with so much love and affection? What would have happened to us if you had not brought us to the ashram? When we spoke to the children here we realized that you had saved us from falling into danger. We feel scared to even think where we would have ended up in Mumbai. Rahul still has wounds on his legs; Karan wakes up every night screaming because of nightmares. They were tortured by the beggar mafia. We were lucky that you brought us here from the railway station. We will confide in Hariharan Uncle. He is the hero of all the children here. They run to him when he comes here and they tell him about school. We too want to talk to Hariharan Uncle.'

The staff called me immediately and I told them that I would come to the ashram the next morning.

When I saw the boys their faces were clear and they seemed relieved that they had decided to tell the truth. Like innocent children who answer the teacher's questions they spoke to me in unison, 'Uncle, we lied to you about our families.' Then they looked at me. I had thought that they would open up to the counsellors as the team was close to all the children, but these boys had chosen me to confide in.

'What we said at the railway station was true. My father is an important official in Tripura. Everyone knows him. You can ask anyone there. If the police know I am here they will take me back immediately.'

Ravi was not boasting when he said this.

'Child, what was the reason you left home in spite

of your father being such an important official?'

Before I could complete my question a volley of words burst from Ravi. He spoke about the humiliation and neglect he had suffered in his joint family. How he was never given any importance, how he was compared to the others and humiliated. How they ignored his dreams and expected him to perform at the level of their expectations in exams. His words conveyed the frustration he had felt at not having the freedom to do what he wanted to do. He sounded sad, angry and helpless. He had decided to leave home, unable to bear the fury of his family when he said he wanted to quit school. Samanth had encouraged him to come to Mumbai. What hurt Ravi most was that he was never acknowledged. Neither of his parents tried to understand or encourage him. That is why the affection he received at the ashram touched him deeply. I understood that it was the first time that anyone had recognized his efforts. Though he had tried to win the affection of his relatives they had ignored him. They did not realize that when they made fun of him, he felt deeply humiliated. There was no one at home to play with him or help him with his studies. Though he lived in a joint family he never experienced the warmth of love even when they ate together. In the eyes of the world he had everything—an illustrious family, an eminent official as a father, big cars, many friends to play with and an array of toys and books. But none of this gave him happiness. He wanted love and affection. I still remember the pain I saw in Ravi's eyes. Though I had not known him for long I felt his pain. What I didn't understand was why families became deserts devoid of affection. If they had bothered to look into Ravi's eyes they would have seen his despair.

I understood that he had put up a brave front to show the world that he did not need the affection he craved. I thought the children would be willing to go home, but surprising me they said, 'We want to go to school here.'

Samanth added, 'Uncle, please help us to stay here. We won't cause any trouble. We will study well and help the other children in their studies.'

I told them that we would find a school after a while. What they needed was time. Time to think about their decisions without being pressurized. Children usually want to return home after the initial burst of excitement. I expected Ravi and Samanth to do the same.

Ravi immersed himself in life at the ashram, working and helping the children with their schoolwork. Samanth also worked in the garden and the farm and Akshay tagged along like a younger brother. They looked relieved that they had told us the truth and now they were enjoying life.

But after a few days when I went to the ashram,

Ravi came to me. He had a slip of paper on which he had written the name and address of his father. I was shocked to read the name. His father was indeed famous. Ravi was right, the police force would be here in no time if they knew that he was in the ashram. I am still surprised that the police didn't locate Ravi. With his father's contacts in the force, they should have been able to trace him. As the police had filed an FIR, all their details were available. A single phone call would have done the trick. Anyway, I rang the number Ravi gave me. What happened next was like the climax of an action movie—a torrent of phone calls, followed by some people and the police coming to the ashram. Perhaps the Mumbai police had given a good report about the ashram as the number of calls from Tripura came down. It was as if the police and Ravi's family were relieved that he was safe.

Who would come to take him? His father? His uncles? I think he was eager to see them. Samanth was excited too. They shared the news with everyone including the cows at the ashram.

They finally arrived—Ravi's parents, two of his uncles and Samanth's mother and brother. I watched them. Ravi's family behaved in a very formal manner. It was as if they were attending a formal function. They looked a bit tense, but they didn't seem like a family.

I felt that the thread of affection that binds a family together had somehow been broken. Samanth's mother and brother were different; it was evident that they had been worried and upset. They looked as if they had regained a treasure when they hugged Samanth. The boys came running when their families arrived. They were no longer the 'big brothers' of the ashram; rather they seemed like small children. Two boys who were overjoyed to meet their parents. Ravi's family seemed more surprised than happy to see him. He had changed a lot from the introvert that he used to be. He spoke confidently and enquired about his relatives; there wasn't a tinge of anger or reproach in his words.

Ravi had never been happy at home; the people there had never been affectionate to him. But it was evident that he had realized the security that his home offered only after he had run away to Mumbai. Samanth too looked eager to go back home. His Mumbai adventure had ended.

Hugging his mother and smiling, Samanth said to me, 'We will come back.' Ravi echoed, 'We will return to visit the ashram.'

The boys took their families around the ashram and introduced everyone. It was after that that I spoke to Ravi's parents. His father looked relieved. Despite being an important official, he sat before me without any airs—he was just Ravi's father then. He never spoke about his powerful position or what he could have done using his contacts. He only requested us to keep Ravi's identity a secret. If the news about Ravi's escapade became known to the public there would be an enquiry by the government. We too knew that it could lead to slander.

But he assured us that Ravi would never need to leave home again. 'I will not lock him up or scare him. I will try to correct the mistakes we made. I will ensure that he is happy at home.'

As he had years of experience in overcoming difficulties, he knew the right solution to this problem. He had to speak to each member of his extended family. There were many dimensions to damage control. I felt that Ravi's leaving home had brought out some changes in his father. He had felt helpless that despite the power and influence he had, he wasn't able to find his son. He knew that this situation could have been avoided if he had paid more attention to Ravi. But he did not blame anyone, neither his wife nor his relatives. Though amid our conversation, he spoke quite harshly to his wife but never blamed her alone. He kept saying, 'We were wrong, we failed as parents.' I had only one answer for him, something that children including Ravi and Samanth had taught me, 'Children can easily understand and adapt to different situations. They are better at this than adults. If you tell them that their parents are busy, they will understand and behave accordingly. But your job shouldn't be a reason to neglect them. They will quickly catch on. You don't need to spend the whole day with them, but you must set apart some time for them. Parents must realize that they have a huge role to play in the character formation of their children. Please don't think that without this care and attention Ravi will be happy in a joint family.'

I told them about Ravi's activities at the ashram, how he taught the children good habits and how he helped them with their schoolwork. They couldn't believe that their son who used to be an introvert had changed so dramatically. I told them that they were lucky to have such a smart son.

Many children like Ravi come from well-to-do families but are very unhappy as they are neglected. Most of them want to run away, but they perhaps lack Ravi's courage and they may not have a friend like Samanth. Will such lonely children grow up to be responsible adults? Our psychologists spoke to the boys' families. They told them about the problems families inadvertently created and how such issues could be resolved. I was sure that Ravi's running away from home would bring out a huge change in his family. His parents would never neglect him. His relatives wouldn't tease or humiliate him. He would be showered with love and affection. The circumstances that had forced a 13-year-old to leave home would change.

Ravi was overcome with happiness. I could see the light that shone in his eyes. He was very excited to go back home. He knew that it was a very different home that awaited him. He wouldn't be mocked or humiliated. His father would make time for him. Whatever happened, his mother would give him priority.

When the boys left, the ashram seemed empty. Akshay was the most affected. For a few days after that he didn't speak to anyone.

Ravi and Samanth never forgot the ashram. They still call us over the phone and keep us updated. They are eager to know about the children at the ashram. They are doing plus two now. Ravi has no problems at school or home. He works hard at school and finds time to help younger children with their studies. It is something he enjoys doing. He gives them tips to build their character and he does it quite naturally. I feel that this is an area where he will work in the future.

All of us are very proud of Ravi and Samanth. We were able to save them from the streets and return them to their families. Their happiness is our reward.

We help children without expecting anything in return. We helped thousands of children without any desire for acknowledgement and that is why an invitation letter from Tripura surprised us. The then Governor of Tripura Padmanabha Balakrishna Acharya gave the ashram an award in acknowledgement of our activities. He described our efforts as 'silent charity'. We received the award. We knew that it was an expression of gratitude from Ravi's family.

The Child Slaves

I still remember that warm evening in 2019. I was in a meeting since morning, talking to some people who had come from Kerala when I got a phone call. It was Remya, who is a senior staff at the ashram. She worked with a team who operated near Kalyan railway station, and was calling from the nearby police station.

'We have two children who speak your language,' Remya said when I answered her call.

'My language?'

'Yes, they don't know either Marathi or Hindi. Please could you come over?'

'My language' that Remya referred to needn't necessarily be Malayalam or Tamil, it could be Kannada or Telugu. Mumbaikars usually refer to anyone who speaks a South Indian language that they don't know as 'south'.

I asked Remya to give the phone to one of the children.

A voice spoke to me in Tamil. It was a voice filled with fear, but all my questions were answered in that tiny, faltering voice. He was Babu, and his cousin Suresh was with him. They had come from Coimbatore. He complained that he had been brought to the police station. He didn't know that Remya had taken them to the police station as part of the formalities we had to follow when we rescued children. We followed protocol unfailingly.

Though I told him not to worry and that it was just a formality he still seemed scared. Then he broke into tears.

'Sir, please help us to go back to Coimbatore. We want to go back now. We can't live here.'

His words were lost in his tears. I could feel the depth of his pain. I did not know what to say to comfort him.

'Don't cry. I will come there right away.' I left the office immediately.

Baiju who had come for the meeting from Kerala accompanied me. He had heard of our foundation for street children and wanted to see us in action. Children who run away from home, arrive in Mumbai after facing many hardships and come here seeking adventure—Baiju wanted to see how we rescued them.

Most people like Baiju have only heard about our ways of rescuing a child—the rehabilitation, taking them back home or to a safe shelter. But all my friends know one thing—saving these children is my life. More than

30,000 children have been given a fresh lease of life by the foundation. The endeavour that I began years ago continues with vigour. It is my destiny to protect desolate children who are separated from their families. My organization tries to heal them mentally as well as physically and we try to mend the broken ties with their families.

The two boys were sitting on a bench in front of the police station when we arrived. It seemed as if they had turned their faces away from what was happening around them, as though they were quarrelling with the world. Remya who was with them introduced me and went to attend to some official work. I sat between the two boys who seemed embodiments of grief. They seemed to be about 15 years old and I felt that I had seen them before. I quickly understood that they were desperate to go back. I had to get to know them better and the best way to do so was our common language.

It usually took 30–45 minutes for the FIR to be prepared and other formalities to be completed when we rescued children and brought them to the police station. It meant that I had this time to spend with the children. I spoke about myself, which means I spoke about the foundation and our activities and how we saved children from the streets. It is not easy to take a conversation forward in such situations, especially when you are in a police station, but I have years of experience in dealing with children. I know what and what not to tell them. As we were talking, a packet of biscuits and a bottle of cold water was brought by a staff member. They seemed to calm down a bit after that. I slowly asked them questions in our mother tongue Tamil. It was Babu who responded. Suresh sat with his head hanging in shame. He didn't even look at me. I knew I had to gain their confidence, then only would they confide in me. I needed to know why they had left home and how they had suffered.

The next step was to take them to a safe shelter. At times they are taken to our temporary shelter at Thane or to the children's home in Ulhasnagar via the children's welfare organization. They are also taken to Swami Vivekananda Manparivartan Kendra, which is run by our organization.

I spoke to them as though I had known them for a long time. They needed care and affection. Though it was evening it was still hot. Even after drinking the cold water we were sweating profusely. Suresh seemed to be in great discomfort. He was twisting and turning on the bench as though his sweat-drenched shirt was hurting him.

Babu started talking to me. It was a story I had heard many times. They had come in search of employment.

They wanted to work and be independent. They had come to Pune hoping for a better life. For them it was not just a dream but a practical decision. They came from a very poor family like the scores of families that eke out a living in Coimbatore. They were not good at studies and did not have any ambition to pursue their education. Babu who was 15 had cleared class 9 and Suresh who was 14 had passed class 8. They had no answer to the question regarding what they would do after completing their education. They had only experienced problems and poverty. Their family led a hand-to-mouth existence. They couldn't even dream of better days. They first heard of Pune when a friend of Babu's father had come to visit them. He was running a small unit that made snacks. When he offered to employ the two boys and pay them well, their families welcomed it. He was a family friend and the boys trusted him. They were happy that they could be together and that the man's children would also be with them. Babu and Suresh did not have to think twice—though they were going to a strange city and did not know the language, they would have each other for company and would be employed. They would be able to eat well and help their families financially. The children of the man from Pune were also on the train with the boys. They had come to Pune six months ago.

'Everything was fine for the first few days,' Babu told me. They were in a unit that made snacks and supplied them to bakeries in Mumbai. It was a small unit. Babu and Suresh were happy as they got enough to eat. They were also allowed to eat the bhujiyas and chips that they made. Their work was also fairly easy, they had to help the older children. They were away from the trials and tribulations their families faced every day; the pressure of studies was also not there. But in a month things changed. Their burden of work increased. They had to work for nearly twelve hours a day. They were no longer considered children. They began working early in the morning, preparing snacks, cleaning the vessels, cutting vegetables, frying the snacks and packing them. They had to clean all the rooms including bathrooms. They had to work through the week. Then slowly their food was also restricted. From three meals a day they were forced to assuage their hunger by eating only what was left over, which were bits of murukku and chips. When they went to sleep on hungry stomachs after a day of hard labour they could only dream of steaming hot rice and curries. The days of hard work without proper food or rest took a toll on their health. Life in Pune became horrible as the man who had brought them there and his children now started showing their true colours.

Once they requested a day off as they wanted to go around the city. They had not gone outside the unit despite having lived there for a few months. Though they didn't know the language they were eager to see the city. But when they made this request they were slapped hard across the face. Babu said, 'I burnt with pain.' Though they had seen fights at home, neither of them had been so brutally beaten up. The child labourers were asked to stay in the room adjacent to the unit. It could hardly be called a room. A 100 square foot space with bunkers where 12 children had to stay. You had no space to yourself. This was their home in Pune, a place to sleep after a long day of hard work.

Babu and Suresh experienced all the difficulties of leaving home. There was no one to comfort them. They had to hold their emotions in check even while they were being tortured. Their problems increased. They didn't have cell phones to call home and were forbidden from borrowing a phone. They had no contact with home during the six months they spent in Pune.

I felt disturbed when I realized that not a single person from their homes enquired about the boys. How could parents be so indifferent when two young boys were living in a strange city? Wouldn't they at least want to hear their voices over the phone? This is something that has always troubled me when I listen to children who run away from home. If only parents paid a little more attention to their children, so many disasters could be averted. Perhaps their circumstances make them behave in this manner. We have no idea what these families go through.

There were other children in the unit that Babu and Suresh were employed in. Most days the two boys received harsh punishments. They were either beaten up or caned, and there was no reason for this punishment. The other boys were also punished brutally; none of them had the courage to complain or protest. They came from underprivileged backgrounds. No one at home even bothered to find out how they were doing. They did not know how to escape so they were in effect imprisoned in the manufacturing unit. The children of the family friend also did not hesitate to use violence on these boys. They had brought Babu and Suresh from Coimbatore. They had taken in the boys and their parents with their polite behaviour and had spoken eloquently about the attractions of the city. Now they found pleasure in torturing the boys. Like their father they became tormentors and the boys lived in fear of them.

One day the man fell ill. His sons had to take up the work of buying the products used for making snacks and preparing and packaging the snacks. They no longer had the time to pay close attention to the children. Babu and Suresh found a way to escape. One day when one of the sons of the owner had gone to the shops, the boys decided to run away. They thought that if they could get to the railway station they could somehow escape. Before anyone could come in search of them they found the railway station and boarded a train to Mumbai. They were anxious to escape and so did not think about how they would survive in a strange city. They had not thought about all this but luckily they ended up in safe hands when they reached Mumbai. Remya, one of our volunteers, was at the railway station on the lookout for unattended children. The difficulties the children had gone through came to an end when Remya took them to the police station. It was the beginning of a new life of hope and peace.

Two staff members of the foundation are always present at each of the five major railway stations in Mumbai. Our teams are especially skilled in identifying runaway children and children who are likely to fall into danger. The foundation has saved nearly 30,000 children. Most of them come from distant states, while some are from nearby districts. There are many reasons why they leave the familiarity and love that home offers and run away to a strange city. It may be due to the cruelties of a stepmother or a great desire for adventure that prompts them to run away from home. Some children have clear goals—they want a job to help their families. Though they don't have any idea about what to do they come to the city in search of employment. For some it is an escape from the poverty at home.

In many stories that I have listened to, the problems were caused by the separation of parents and the cruelties of the stepfather or stepmother and their older children. But some come to Mumbai for quite a different reason. They are lured by the glittering world of cinema and the glamour of the city. But what awaits them in this city are dangers of different kinds. In very little time their dreams are destroyed. Life on the streets isn't colourful—it is filled with traps and danger. The city and the people here wound the minds and bodies of such children—wounds that last a lifetime. Along with their hopes their childhood too comes to an end. It requires a lot of effort to bring these children out of the deep trauma they experience. We have to help them to overcome this and move forward.

I am saying all this neither because I lead a team that saves children nor because I have interacted with more than 10,000 children. I say this because I was a runaway child myself. I have run away from home not once but thrice. The strength I gained from surviving on these streets alone fuels my endeavour. My life's mantra, my destiny is to save these children from the streets and ensure that they are safe.

As I sat with Babu on the bench in front of the police station and listened to him, I was thinking about myself when I was his age. I was 15 when I came to Mumbai without any money. I had no friends here either. But I had the confidence that I would be able to survive in this strange city. Like these boys I too was all alone in this city. My home was far away. Suresh seemed a little less nervous after Babu had finished telling me how they reached Mumbai. He too started responding to my questions. I felt they were relaxing as someone was speaking to them in Tamil in an affectionate manner. They started speaking confidently.

I then spoke to them about the next step. After the formalities at the police station were over it was our responsibility to take them to a safe shelter and then to send them back home. If their parents came here they could go back with them or the children would be sent home with the police.

'We will inform your parents. We will see if they can come here; anyhow you will be home within a week.'

Though Babu nodded his head, Suresh looked upset. He hung his head, looking despondent. I could see him fall into the depths of sorrow as if he would never escape from Mumbai. He started to cry.

'I won't stay here. I want to go to Coimbatore. I want to go now. Can't anyone help us?' he said between tears.

I could understand his feelings. It was sheer luck that they had escaped. They could have still been trapped in that manufacturing unit in Pune, suffering mental and physical torture. Though they had escaped, Suresh didn't feel comfortable among strangers. The Tamil I spoke and the words of affection I uttered comforted him, but he was still distraught. He just wanted to go home. I knew that none of the reasons that prompted him to leave home six months ago would be in his mind now.

When we save a child from the streets our work is not over, rather it just begins. The organization helps them to overcome the trauma they have experienced and equips them to move forward. The astute staff of the Street Children Foundation speak to the children in great detail. We not only get information about their families but also get to know their dreams and ambitions. We help them pursue their dreams and speak to their families to sort out the problems they have faced. We try to remove any possibility of the children leaving home again.

I tried to explain all this to Suresh, but he continued to weep. As I could not comfort him no matter how much I tried I did something I never do—something we tell our team members never to do. I called his people on my mobile phone. I broke my own rule that we had to use the official phone to call the families of runaway children. It was his plight that had forced me to do so. But that single phone call triggered dramatic events that lasted for several days. I later felt that I should not have made that call. It led to many unexpected events, though I didn't realize it then. I could hear Suresh talking to his father. The conversation shocked me. It was only then that I got to know of the extent of the torture that the 'family friend' had inflicted on the two boys. Suresh's words convinced me that it was an attack that the boys had faced. A criminal offence had been committed. A man and his sons had brought two children to Mumbai promising employment and wages and then had exploited the boys. I was unable to contain my anger and sorrow and my emotions were clearly visible on my face.

Seeing my expression Babu lifted Suresh's collar, showing me his back. I was dumbstruck. He had been caned mercilessly. His back was covered with red marks. I understood what he had not been able to tell me. It was the mark of the punishments he had received. His body bore evidence of violence worse than what is shown on screen in movies. There were six or seven red weals on his back and two of them were bleeding.

I couldn't even imagine the pain the boy was going through. I realized that this was what made him writhe as he sat on the bench in the police station sweating from the heat. The salty sweat drops must have worsened the pain. It was terrible to watch his discomfort. After seeing the wounds on Suresh's body I wondered about Babu's condition. Was he too whipped or had he managed to escape this punishment? I immediately realized that Babu hadn't been lucky. The wounds were on his legs. Some of them had healed, others were fresh. There were marks on his feet as well. I felt pained but at the same time I was furious. I have seen people who behave without an atom of kindness. They are not kind towards workers or children. It is quite common to see faces darkened with pain in places where such people have power. I have often felt that they are more cruel to helpless children. Men and women who torture children deserve to be punished severely. No kindness should be shown to such people.

Babu and Suresh talked to their parents for a long time. It was as if they couldn't stop telling them of the pain they had suffered. As I listened to them I could feel anger and sorrow rise within me. These boys needed help. Their wounds had to be treated and they needed counselling. I could not allow them to stay in a strange place suffering from pain, their minds filled with anxiety. They needed the safety of a home. I decided to take them to our centre in Mamnoli from the police station.

'Try to forget the past. You will be able to go back

to Coimbatore soon. Think about the good things that are going to happen. Be optimistic.' I repeated this till it was time for me to go back to my office.

I made sure that all the formalities at the police station had been completed. I gave instructions to the team members. I saw that Babu and Suresh were slowly recovering their ability to smile and laugh. They went along with Remya talking about their telephone conversations. Baiju too accompanied them. I needed to make sure that these boys would never have to leave home again. They needed to be safe at home till they completed their studies and found employment. I had to speak to their parents personally. I decided to meet them when they came to Mumbai. But little did I know then of the torrent of phone calls that would flow on my mobile phone.

My phone rang at 6 p.m. and it didn't stop ringing after that. All the calls were from Coimbatore. The boys' parents, uncles and relatives kept calling to find out how Babu and Suresh were. All of them wanted to speak to the boys. They asked me whether I would bring them to Coimbatore by air, or whether they would be put on a train. I received a volley of instructions. Though I told them that there were certain formalities to be completed, they didn't seem to understand. The calls kept pouring in and I had to repeat myself several times.

I kept telling them, 'The children are safe but they are not with me now. They are at an ashram a few kilometres away. I will give you the phone number of the ashram and you can talk to the boys. The police have prepared the FIR, you can come here and take them back.' I had to repeat the same thing each time someone called from Coimbatore. Finally I had to cut the call. But what surprised me was that not one of them spoke about the family friend who had tortured them. It was as though they were trying to evade the topic.

I told everyone who called me to file a complaint against this man who had tortured Babu and Suresh, but none of them was willing to talk about him. The next day too the phone calls continued, but after giving them the phone number of the ashram I did not attend any more calls. The ashram told me that the boys' wounds had been dressed and they were being taken care of.

But the next day I received another call, an official call. He introduced himself as the sub-inspector of the Pune police station. 'There is a complaint against you that you have two boys with you and are not allowing them to leave. If you don't let them go, I will file a case against you.' He spoke in an authoritative tone.

'Who has filed this case?' I asked very calmly.

He didn't answer me; he kept saying that unless I let the boys go he would file a case against me. I knew where this was leading. Without allowing him to continue, I said, 'Thank you, I will call back.' Though the man called again I didn't answer.

I informed my team in Pune. They found that he was indeed the SI but he had not called from his official phone number. I had been working with children for several years now, but I had never been accused of kidnapping before. Though I felt a bit disturbed I decided to ignore this complaint. But what transpired the next day made me change my decision to not involve the police in this matter. My friends and business contacts started ringing me. They told me that a police officer from Pune had been ringing them to find out details regarding my business and my home. I had not expected this. What right did he have to trouble my friends and acquaintances? I told everyone who called me that these enquiries were with regard to the charity work I did for children. But I was seething with anger. I decided to call him.

'I am Hariharan. What is your name?' I began the conversation. Informing him that I was recording our conversation, I told him in detail about the foundation for street children. 'The case you are talking about, an FIR has been filed. I can send you a copy.' There was no answer.

I continued, 'If you hold on I will put the assistant commissioner on the line.' That decided matters. He said, 'No, all that isn't needed,' and hung up. I was sure that the 'family friend' had begun to work. He wanted to get the boys back. I called Babu's and Suresh's parents.

'Are you crazy to file such a complaint?' I was furious. 'I rescued your children, I took them to a safe shelter and you are accusing me of being a kidnapper?'

They were apologetic. 'The man told us that you had taken the boys away and he had filed a complaint against you to get them back. We tried calling you, but you didn't answer.'

I assured them that the boys were safe. I also told them that I would file a case against the 'family friend' and the police officer in Pune. After that things fell in place. The parents decided to come to Mumbai in two days. We too started making preparations to send the boys home.

I received another call, this time the caller spoke in Marathi. It was a threatening phone call asking me to beware. I wasn't surprised, I was used to getting such calls. When I told him that I was recording the call he stopped talking. To be honest I didn't think about any of this in the next few days. I was extremely happy to see Babu and Suresh become normal. Their stay at the ashram energized them. Their wounds healed. Like other teenagers, they too started talking and playing games. Suresh, who had been quite silent, changed dramatically.

His face reflected his happiness. They mingled with the other children at the ashram.

Their parents arrived from Coimbatore and we took them straight to the ashram. Their reunion touched me deeply. Despite working for so many years in this field I still feel touched when I watch children meeting their parents after leaving home.

But there was a question I asked Suresh's father.

'Why didn't you call him even once in the past six months?'

The man bowed his head.

'I trusted my friend. He told me that the boys were fine. Whenever we called, he would say that the children were playing or that they were away somewhere and he couldn't call them. We too believed that they were happy.'

'But how could you trust him so blindly? Your 14-year-old son was living in a strange city without even knowing the language that is spoken here. How could you go for six months without talking to him in this age of mobile phones?' He had no answer. I told him that I would file a case against their family friend in Pune and that I needed only Suresh's statement to do so. He didn't object. He seemed relieved after going around the ashram and being informed of our activities. I noticed that the father and son did not display affection; they had a very formal relationship. They didn't even hug each other on meeting after six months. I felt that there was no friendship between them.

They prepared to leave for Coimbatore. I told the children to continue their studies. It was their future and they shouldn't compromise at any cost. I promised to help them find some employment in Coimbatore after they finished their education.

After speaking to Suresh about his family, I realized there was some problem. He told me, 'My father has two wives.' Both the wives stayed in the same house and quarrels were the norm. This was one reason that made him want to leave home. He might have felt that though in a strange city, he could live in peace away from all the troubles at home. The turbulent atmosphere at home made Suresh become close to Babu. He confided in Babu and spent most of his time at his house. He ate with his friend and slept undisturbed away from the quarrels that erupted at home.

I asked them about Babu's home. Suresh said, 'Babu is lucky. There aren't any problems in his house. He can go back to school.'

His words made a deep impact on me. Children were very observant and quite accurate in their assumptions. Most often parents do not realize this. Children have a knack for tackling problems. Their stay at Pune had changed Suresh and Babu a lot. I was sure that with a little encouragement they would easily succeed in life.

I promised Suresh that I would try to make things better at his home. I would talk to his father about the quarrels and how disturbing it was to the boy. I would support him to change his ways. We could also talk to his mother and make her aware of what she was doing. I promised to financially support him if he wanted to move to a hostel in order to study. He promised me that he would continue his education.

I told them to work hard, be active in sports and be positive all the time.

Suresh's father promised me that there would be no reason for the boys to leave home. The families realized that it was dangerous to send their young children believing the words of a 'friend' to a strange city for employment. They understood that this would be dangerous for young children.

They were lucky as they got the boys back. Thousands of families still wait for their children who have disappeared into the streets after leaving home. I am waiting to see the boys succeed. Their wounds will heal and the scars will fade. They will be more positive in their attitude after having gone through a turbulent experience. They will be kinder. They will be the first to help a child stranded on the road. They will never forget how cruel people can be to children who do not know anything other than play. They will know the value of kindness and sympathy. I have traversed this distance as a child. I know what they feel. I speak from the conviction of my experiences—there is a better tomorrow, for everyone.

Baiju came to see me from Kerala again. The first question that he asked me was about the 'family friend' from Pune who had tortured the boys.

'He is in jail and it won't be easy for him to escape,' I said. Baiju closed his eyes for a while and then said, 'Well done!'

Still Missing

I was driving through D.N. Road. My wife Harneet was with me. It was nearing twilight and the roads were busy. I suddenly stepped on the brake. I still remember the curses showered on me by a bike rider who had to swerve to avoid hitting me as I jumped out of the car.

I leaped onto the footpath and ran in the opposite direction. I called out to a boy wearing black jeans and a red shirt who was sitting on a bike fixed on its stand. He didn't hear me and I called louder and this time he lifted his head, but it was not because he had seen me. He was smiling at his friend. He started the bike and it was then that I saw his face. I had been mistaken. It was only then I took notice of the pavement that had shops selling mobile accessories, CDs and books. I returned to my car and heard people cursing me as my car was blocking the traffic. I was focusing on driving when I became aware of my surroundings. Harneet looked at me. I said, 'I thought it was Manikanth.' She patted my shoulder and I felt tears welling up in my eyes.

I had behaved like this before, imagining I had spotted him. I drove in silence. I noticed only the children as my car moved along the road. Humans have a long period of childhood. It takes around 20 years for a human being to become a social being after receiving care and affection from parents and the skills to navigate the world around them.

I make time for my own children. I adapt my routine to the changes that come over their life as they grow up. I don't know how many of us can do that. I wish that every child would benefit from such care. I am always conscious of my surroundings, whether I am in a car or the metro or even when I am on my morning walk. I am always on the lookout for children who need help. When I feel that a child needs help I go up and speak to them. Many people have accused me of interfering in the lives of others and some have even called the police.

I first heard of Manikanth when I was speaking to my daughter. She wanted to study abroad after completing her schooling. So I used to reach home before five in the evening. If I could, I would pick her up from school at 3.30 and make her a light snack. If I had a meeting in the evening, I would cook dinner for her before I left. She would soon leave home to pursue her studies in a foreign country. Then she wouldn't have time for me so I wanted to spend as much time as I possibly could with her. Thus, I used to spend most of my time at home during those days.

It was evening when I received a WhatsApp message. It was a photograph.

'Hari, this Hyderabad cutie pie has arrived.' The message was from Sidwi Sarve.

Glancing at the photo I typed, 'He is not a cutie pie.'

'No, uncle. Come here and see for yourself.'

Sidwi was not someone who made rash comments. She had been involved in the area of children's rights much before I started working in the same field. She had come for the book release of *Runaway Children*. She was a Miss India runner-up then. She had to go through some harrowing experiences that upset her emotional balance. But it made her capable of engaging in charity activities for children even while doing a full-time job. She is an excellent counsellor now, though she stays away when she has mood swings.

Sidwi first met Manikanth at a temporary shelter. We got him from Chhatrapati Shivaji Terminus. When our volunteers found him cowering in a corner of an empty compartment of a train from Hyderabad, he looked like a pile of rags. It was difficult to comprehend that it was a small child. Our volunteers brought him to the platform and gave him food and water. He did not say a word and then they brought him to the shelter. They bathed him, cut his hair and gave him a pair of shorts and a T-shirt. They gave him food again. He was still silent. He didn't tell us who he was or where he had come from. He sat dazed. You could fathom the pain he had gone through from his blank stare, but Sidwi felt some hidden power in his eyes that were otherwise filled with sorrow. She felt more affection for him than she usually felt towards such children. That is why she called him 'cutie pie'.

We know the dangers children land up in. So we try to make them feel safe and secure when they are with us without trying to probe into their past. He wasn't interested in exploring the city or even stepping out of the place. We knew that it was not a teenager's quest for adventure that had brought him to Mumbai.

Sidwi treated him like a long-lost friend. He too warmed up to her. She continued to make him feel safe without asking any questions, waiting for his wounds to heal.

He slowly started conversing with us. He had no parents, only an aged grandmother. Food was scarce at home and he had come in search of a job.

We did not take his story at face value. He may not have been lying about his family, but there was a pattern in his story that runaway children usually follow. We knew that if we questioned him he would retreat into silence.

Two days later he said that he had left home to go to Chennai. When he reached the railway station, a train to Mumbai was at the platform. His friends had told him that he could travel without a ticket provided he hid when the ticket checker came. Nobody came to check the tickets. He did not even get a drop of water. He was scared to leave the train when it stopped and he had fallen asleep in the compartment.

When Sidwi asked him whether his grandmother would worry about him he said that she didn't even like him and that she wouldn't come looking for him. He was staring at something in the distance when he told Sidwi this. When she asked him if he had any other relatives, he evaded the question.

She gave him time to recover. Maybe when he gained courage he would tell her all about himself and she also felt that maybe he was telling her the truth.

I saw him very briefly during this time. Mostly Sidwi was with him.

She asked him, 'Won't your school ask someone why you are not attending class?'

He laughed. 'No one goes to school regularly. Most of the children work or sit at home. I used to work in a mill and in a company that packages clothes.'

'Don't you have any relatives?' I asked him.

He closed his eyes and smiled in answer.

We had to find his grandmother and make arrangements for him to continue in his old school, if that was not possible we would have to get him admission to a school in Mumbai. He would have to be taken to the ashram from the shelter. I felt that being with the children in the ashram and the atmosphere there would give him the courage to speak the truth.

I thought of the smile that had flashed in his eyes the day I met him. Beyond the lie or truth that lay hidden in his smile, there was a request for friendship. He looked smart in his new shorts and T-shirt. I caught a glimpse of myself in his eyes. There was a photograph taken when I was in class 7, but I could convince people that I was in class 10 as I had a look of maturity that belied my age. I saw that in him too. After meeting him I too felt close to him like Sidwi did.

We took him to the ashram. Though he quickly befriended the children, we noticed that he would often withdraw into himself and sit silently. He had been sexually abused not once but many times. There were wounds on his body. He was in pain when he walked. The doctor gave us his medical report and prescribed medicines for his wounds. Medicines could heal his wounds but what about his emotions? Only time, kindness and love could make him better.

Within a week he shone as a volunteer.

Sidwi asked me, 'See? I guessed right, didn't I?'

I agreed, 'He is a cutie pie.'

He gained everyone's love in no time and became a star in the ashram. Children would obey all his orders. He looked very different now. There was something very attractive about him.

He loved to sing and dance. He would even ride the cows as though they were horses. He acted as if he were returning victorious from a battle. He would sing a triumphant tune and that would be the moment he fell from the back of the cow. But he would make that into a comic scene. We were all Manikanth fans.

Sidwi still watched him closely especially when he retreated into silence. This was a pattern we found in sexually abused children. They constantly try to erase their past, but it continues to trouble them like a poisoned thorn. Sidwi made it a point to spend more time with him. Gradually they started conversing. He told her that he had parents but that he did not want to go back home. Though he was happy at the ashram, our policy was to send children home if possible. Children need the love and protection of their homes. So even if Manikanth was happy in the ashram, we needed to make sure that he returned home and grew up with his people around him. But our policy was to create a conducive atmosphere for him to live in the ashram and pursue his studies till he told us about his family and expressed a desire to go back to them. One of our main aims is to allow children to reach a position where they make the right decisions about their own lives. Around 80 per cent of the children who come to us want to go home within a week. We take the rest to the ashram. We enrol them in a carefully structured course that lasts for 45 days, which is for them to feel rejuvenated. As they do this course filled with games, laughter and yoga, there comes a palpable change in the children. They begin to think about themselves and society.

There are around 30 children in the ashram at a time. It is usually when they are playing that a family comes in to take their child home, which is a shock for the others. The laughter and games stop. We too feel bad when we see this. We too become silent. Seeing this, some of the children would say, 'I too want to go home.'

Forty-five days had passed since Manikanth had arrived at the ashram. He was one of us now. We had decided on a date to hold the 'See-off' function at the ashram. This was a function that was held twice or thrice a year. Ministers, educationists, social workers, police and artists attend this function, which is also open to the people of the city. It is an opportunity for the children to reunite with their parents. The children showcase their talents. It is a day when our well-wishers and the people in the neighbourhood come together with dedication and joy. Thousands of children return home every day from our institutions but we don't publish this news. This function is held to create social awareness.

The children started practising dance and music two weeks before the programme was scheduled. The costumes were ready. Travel bags with toothpaste, brush, towels and clothes were packed for those children who were leaving with their parents. Manikanth was busy as the main star and the organizer. The day of the function arrived. There were glittering lights everywhere.

He was constantly by my side the whole day. Sidwi clicked many pictures of him. He was her pet student. He performed brilliantly.

He watched his friends who had been with him leave with their parents, holding my hand with a blank expression on his face.

No one had come for him. I wondered whether he too wanted to see his parents. But he was calling each child who was leaving by name and waving goodbye to them. It was as though he was leading them in their happiness. I could feel my heart filling with love for him. I felt that he had been born in the ashram and had grown up there. I must find a school for him and he should continue his studies. He had learnt Hindi. Perhaps Mumbai was his place; perhaps he was destined to be by my side. Such thoughts filled me as I drove back home. I called Sidwi when I got home to ask whether there was any change in Manikanth after the function. She had been watching him closely. She said that despite his enthusiasm and vigour she had noticed his silence. But she thought that it was a positive change. She told me that she was hoping he would start thinking about his home after the function. I too felt inclined to think the same. We agreed to leave it to time to decide.

The next week I had to go to Hyderabad to attend some meetings regarding business matters. I did not have time to visit the ashram before I left. It was blistering hot in Hyderabad and I had back-to-back meetings. The moment I finished my work I booked the night flight to Mumbai. I was packing my bag thinking that I would rest in Mumbai when Sidwi rang me.

'I rang you but you didn't respond,' she said.

'I saw your calls but I was busy. I thought I would call you after I came back. Why, is there anything urgent?'

Not allowing me to continue, she shouted, 'Hari Uncle, there is a breakthrough. He wants to go home now. He has a family in Hyderabad. We traced them. He wants to study and he wants to go back to his old school. We are bringing him to Hyderabad tomorrow. I am coming too. Please cancel your flight.'

I was taken aback. She never left Mumbai. She

avoided journeys due to her mood swings. Now she was coming here.

Our volunteers go through complex emotional states each time they deal with a child. Though they want the child to be with them due to the great love they share, the moment the child says that he wants to back to his family they are eager to reunite the family. That is an experience that moulds our lives.

When a child tells us that he wants to go home and we are not able to trace the address that he has given us, the child welfare committee takes up the process. They take the child home accompanied by the police and entrust the social service agencies in the vicinity to monitor the child's home.

Now Sidwi was requesting me, 'Hari Uncle, cancel your flight. Stay there for one more day. We will take him home.'

It was the first time that she had made such a request. I cancelled my flight. I met the representatives of the child welfare committee in Hyderabad the next day. They had to complete the paperwork. I went along with them to the railway station. Manikanth got down from the train and hung onto my arm. He kept talking about his journey, the sights he had seen, the food he ate, the people in the compartment and the herd of goats that had passed by when the train had stopped.

When the crowd on the platform dwindled we went out and got into a taxi to go to the office of the child welfare committee.

'Let's eat something,' I said. We had lunch together. I offered him a laddoo and Sidwi bought him a multi-coloured ice cream. He did not eat the ice cream; he just played with the colours, dipping the spoon into the bowl. I also took him to the mall with my staff members. It helped him to make friends with them. I wanted him to get to know the members of the regional office. Then we went to the office of the child welfare committee. It was a platform for him to speak in Telugu. Meanwhile, he went and had a bath and after that we left the office. But fear filled his eyes as we walked towards the car. I held him close and told him not to worry. 'We will just go to your home and see what the situation is, that is all. We will decide what to do later.'

He relaxed a bit and cracked a joke in Telugu and told us the way home.

'Let us go to the railway station. Then we turn left. I will show you the way.'

We got into the car, but when we reached the railway station he changed his plans.

'Let us go to my school first. I live near the school. My teachers will take me home. The road to my house is narrow; you can't get there in a car. So you don't need to bother.'

Sidwi and I looked at each other. Rules do not allow us to hand him over to the teachers.

I said, 'Come, let us go to your school.'

He told us the way with a show of enthusiasm. Sitting in the small space between the driver and me he gave us directions, taking control. He knew every nook and corner of that area.

Our car drove into the compound, passing the melee of students as they were leaving school. The school was in a small compound in an old building with pictures drawn on the walls. He jumped out even before the car stopped. Before we could get down he dragged a teacher towards us and disappeared into the crowd of students. The children were pulling at his bag and new clothes, showing their affection. Undoubtedly he was a hero there. The teachers told us that he had never created trouble in school. He was never disobedient and was always active.

But why didn't they enquire when he didn't come to school for so many days?

He lived close to the school, didn't anyone say anything?

We questioned them. But they did not seem to realize the seriousness of our questions. They said that they did not know his parents and seemed to evade responsibility.

We were confused as he had told us that his teachers would take him home. We met the headmaster, a very mild-mannered man. He said that Manikanth had run away from home twice before and had come back by himself. That is why his family had not bothered to find him. He told us the way to Manikanth's home. 'Most of the children here are like this. What can I do?' the headmaster said.

As we walked out, Sidwi whispered that Manikanth knew almost every railway station in Andhra. When the train had entered Andhra he began calling out the name of each station. It was clear that he had run away from home before.

We wanted to visit his parents and speak to them. We wanted to make sure he would be safe. We couldn't leave Manikanth who had won us over with his vivacity by just completing the formalities. Sidwi and I decided that we would make sure that he wouldn't leave home again. There may have been a case filed at the police station and we would have to settle that also.

We took the route the headmaster told us and reached a slum. It was a narrow path and we filled it as we moved forward. We turned a corner and there were six to seven houses in a row. His house was right at the edge. Beyond that was a field. The children hooted with joy when they saw Manikanth. They said, 'You look stylish. Where were you?' They followed us with their questions. Suddenly he moved and stood behind me using me as a shield. He held my shirt tight and slowed his pace.

We saw his house. Hearing the noise a shabbily dressed woman came out. As we moved closer a young man, about 20 years of age, came out and stood next to her. His stance reminded me of the actors who played the youth of hardened villains. I felt a tremor run through Manikanth's hands. I knew that this woman wasn't his mother and that the man had raped him.

'Done! Done! Done!' I told myself.

I told him, 'Don't worry my child, there is no problem, it is decided—you are not staying here.'

I could feel his fear recede. He stopped shivering. He repeated, 'No problem.'

He had picked up some words in English.

The woman was his stepmother who had no affection towards the boy.

We decided to wait for his father. Without speaking to anyone, we stood gazing at the fields for an hour. Then his father came; he was a gardener. I said to the local volunteer, 'You tell him.'

'You scoundrel, you married again and now you

watch. Your wife's son is going to be arrested under a non-bailable warrant.'

His father began to wail. 'Please pardon me, it won't happen again. I will take care of him.' He fell at our feet.

We told him that Manikanth wouldn't stay there. He would be in a hostel under our protection. 'On Sundays, he will eat lunch with you accompanied either by one of our volunteers or by his teacher. What do you say? We won't file a case.'

He was quite ignorant of what had happened. He folded his hands before us.

Two months later, I got a call from the child welfare committee.

'Sir, are you free?' the voice sounded scared.

'Tell me,' I said.

'Sir, there is a problem. He has run away again.'

I am still disturbed by his absence and tracking him even now on his father's behalf, based on a complaint filed by his father as a third party can't track a child.

Where had he gone? When would his wounds heal?

The Economist

The first thing I noticed about him was his smile. It was a smile that overflowed from his face lighting up the entire room. He did not show any nervousness even though he was among strangers. A very pleasant child with a positive attitude is what I thought. We see children who spend even a day on the streets in Mumbai tremble in fear when they reach us. This was a change from the norm. Children feel nervous after leaving the familiarity of home. Some of them are excited at the adventure of a new place and new people in the initial days. But this changes quickly. If they have to live on the streets for long, the shine on their faces fade just as their clothes become shabby. We can sense the anxiety in their eyes.

But he was different.

He behaved as if he had come to our office while playing with his friends or on his way to watch a movie. He wore a pair of brown pants and a shirt with black stripes. His shoes though old were neat. He wasn't nervous at having left home, he seemed eager for the next adventure. Nothing seemed to faze him, neither the place nor the strangers around him.

Why do I still remember him after all these years? My memories of him are still fresh. I remember everything from the time he came to our office till he left us two months later.

Was it because I was like him in my childhood? I saw in him the same characteristics I had had as a child, in the way he spoke and in his perspectives. After a while I realized that we shared the same opinion on several matters. I too had behaved like him when I came to Mumbai as a teenager. I had a 'don't care,' attitude and was confident to face life in a strange city. Life is strange—we had the same dreams, the same thoughts.

I was busy attending a meeting at the Thane office. It was then that a staff member brought him along. He had been alone at the railway station. He was from Odisha and knew a smattering of Hindi. But language wasn't a barrier for him. He spoke incessantly and joked with our staff. He waited for me till my meeting was over. He only had a small bag with him. As it was the monthly meeting of the Foundation, it was an hour before the meeting concluded. There were many matters to be discussed in great detail. I was watching him even as the meeting went on. The smile was always on his face. He was listening to us and he even smiled at me when he caught me looking at him.

We have rescued many children who arrive alone in Mumbai from railway stations and bus terminals—children who are called runaways by society. He was very different from them. He was a smart boy, I thought to myself. I had to attend a lot of phone calls during the meeting. I was speaking about children, my business and about shares and the market as I invest in shares.

After the meeting I went to him and he asked me in Hindi, 'Boss, are you into trading?'

It was an unexpected question. 'I invest in shares. Do you know the market?' I asked him.

'I was listening to you. It is interesting to study about shares and the share market,' he said.

I had never met a child who discussed the share market with me, and neither had any boy spoken with such confidence with me on the first meeting.

I wondered who had run away from home. Was it him or me? I felt as if I were the child who had gone to him for help. He was that confident. His Hindi wasn't very fluent. He didn't know Marathi. Odia was his mother tongue and he knew a little Bengali. But that was more than enough for him.

Who was this boy and why had he come to Mumbai?

I will tell you what he told us in brief.

'My name is Sohan. I live in Cuttack in Odisha. I'm 15 and I am in class 10. My parents are no more. I live with my grandmother. She works in houses nearby and that is how we get by. She takes good care of me. But a few days ago she fell ill. She can't go to work anymore and that is why I came to Mumbai. I have to find some work and send money home. I don't remember my parents; my grandmother brought me up. She taught me to be independent. She asked me to always dress neatly. She told me that no matter what happened I shouldn't appear in public in a dishevelled state. She told me to behave well as first impressions are important. We live in a small rented house but we keep it clean. We live in a place that is packed with houses and so I have many friends. Most of them are my age but very few of them attend school. They work in a factory nearby but they are not paid well. They advised me to come to Mumbai and work as the pay is better here. I have no work experience. I just help my grandmother in washing and drying clothes and then folding them neatly; I can clean the house, make khichdi and wash the utensils. I am willing to do anything in Mumbai. I am only sad that I can't study. I used to do well in school. My teachers are very fond of me. They tell me that I must go to college, pass my exams and get a government job. I too want to go to college. Maths is my favourite subject. I do arithmetic in my head. It is like a game. I buy the groceries for home.

'When the shopkeeper begins to calculate—wheat 11, oil 20, pulses 14, onions 15, then some vegetables—I interrupt him telling him that it is ₹79 and he has to return ₹21 as I hand him a hundred-rupee note. The shopkeeper tells me that I am very smart. Many people tell me that I can be a maths teacher in a school and if I study more I can even teach in a college. Then I will get paid well and I will be able to buy a house or a car. But I want to be a businessman. I may sell groceries or clothes or food. I may make food and sell it in all the food outlets in Bhubaneswar. It won't be the way some people make pickles and papads at home and sell them to nearby shops and houses. I want a business that has people and machines working in factories day and night. I want to be a successful businessman and that is why I have come to Mumbai. I didn't run away from home.'

After telling me his story Sohan smiled. He looked like a child who had read out a story he had written for a school competition or a children's magazine and was waiting for my opinion. His expression told me that he was quite proud of the story he had told me. Perhaps it was a story he had created to tell anyone who asked him why he was in Mumbai. It was a story with no loopholes and it explained why he had come to Mumbai.

He smiled as if he had enjoyed his own story. He seemed to be happy as everyone had now heard his story; the happiness of a person who has nothing but this story.

Most children don't tell us the truth about themselves when we first meet them. They usually tell us that their parents are dead and that they live with their grandmother/grandfather. They never divulge the details about their family. Though they pretend to be brave they never tell us what they are scared of. We watch them and then we understand that they are afraid of loud noises, of darkness, of the smell of cigarettes, smoke or of heights. Most children are very scared. Though they laugh and joke, they are emotionally disturbed. Even a kind word from a stranger can make them weep. I knew that I couldn't get a clear idea about Sohan after speaking to him only once. Anyway, this boy had big dreams and that was good. I decided to deal with the other things later.

We needed to find a place for Sohan to stay. He could stay at Swami Vivekananda Manparivartan Kendra run by the foundation. There were a few children we had rescued from the streets at the ashram. Sohan could stay there and continue his studies. He wouldn't miss classes till we located his family. But language was a problem. As he didn't know Hindi or Marathi it would be difficult for him to study in a school in Mumbai. Sohan heard us discussing him. He realized that we were thinking about sending him to Odisha. His attitude changed. He started crying. 'Don't send me back. I will learn Hindi. Put me in a school here, don't send me back.'

He seemed very worried; anyway we decided to put him up at the ashram for a few days. It would help him recover from his troubling experiences. If he had suffered at home or school he would need time to recover.

Sohan began to stay in the ashram. I forgot about him for a while. The staff introduced him to the way of life at the ashram. From their reports I understood that he had settled in well. I saw him when I visited the ashram. He came running to me as I got out of my car. He was excited and shot a volley of questions. 'How are you? How is the business? Do you know what I have been doing here? Don't you want to meet my friends?' He walked along with me and was by my side when I walked around the campus and spoke to the other children. He did not leave me even when I sat down for the usual meeting with the staff. He sat listening carefully to us, his smile never leaving his face.

He was friends with everyone, with children of all age groups. He was particularly fond of very young children. He could play with them for any length of time. After playing, he would wander around the campus. He seemed free from worries. I asked his friends whether he was putting on an act for me or if this was his usual behaviour. The boys were eager to talk about Sohan.

'He is very active. He is either talking or singing. I teach him Hindi and he helps me with maths and science. I guess I will soon pick up Odia and Bengali,' Amir, a 15-year-old, said. Sohan and he had become good friends.

One of the staff told me, 'In a book, he has written down the cost of the groceries that we buy for the ashram. He often goes through that book.'

I was curious to see the book and soon it was in my hands. It was filled with columns, figures and notes. He had written in Odia. It seemed like a grocer's ledger. He had written down everything that was bought from the day he came to the ashram with the dates.

What was this all about?

Our supervisor smiled, 'He writes down the cost of everything we buy; milk, pulses, vegetables, oil. He reads the cost of these items in the newspapers and the cost written on the packets. Then he wants to know how much the shop charged us. He asks the other children about the cost of these items in their native places. He has written down all that. I have never seen a child like him.'

No wonder Sohan wanted to be a businessman when he grew up. He had already started preparing for it. It is very rare for young children to have such clear-cut goals in life. Though he told me about his interest in the share market the day we met, it was astonishing to see the meticulous way in which he had written down the accounts.

I asked him, 'What have you written? Are you planning to send a report to the government on the cost of groceries?'

Sohan smiled. 'I was comparing the cost of groceries. At home I used to do the shopping. So I know how much each thing costs, I was curious to know the cost of these things in a city like Mumbai. I can also see how much the prices go up each day. The cost of vegetables goes up every day. If we expand our vegetable garden, we can cut costs.'

He told me that this was his favourite hobby when he was in Cuttack. He wrote down the cost of items and compared the costs with those of other days. I knew that whatever happened, his love for maths would continue throughout his life.

But he never said anything about his family. He always evaded such questions. If we repeatedly asked him he would reply, 'I don't even remember my parents,' and walk away.

We know children well. They will decide when they want to talk about something. I expected Sohan to talk about his family after a few days at the ashram, or open up to the counsellors or his friends. But nothing of the sort happened in the first month. He was happy in the ashram and quickly adapted to our ways. He made more friends and explored the ashram. He continued to maintain his book of accounts.

The supervisor is at the ashram day and night, and he quickly notices if a child is unwell, either physically or mentally. He is able to identify children who have been abused or neglected. He is hardly ever mistaken. He did not find anything amiss with Sohan. We decided to give him a month before taking a decision regarding his schooling.

Sohan wished to join a school in Mumbai. He often reminded me, 'I am learning Hindi.' He watched Hindi movies with Amir and quickly picked up words and sentences. He would try his new vocabulary out with the people in the ashram. He picked up the language and was able to even read and write in Hindi. The ease with which he had become fluent in Hindi impressed us and he became a star at the ashram.

Whenever I visited the ashram he would be by my side asking questions. His questions ranged from the latest news about NIFTY to the cost of milk in Kerala. There was hardly any topic that did not interest him and so it was quite a task to answer his questions.

It was only later that we realized that beneath his pleasant demeanour, he was a bit troubled. One day when I went to the ashram, Sohan was nowhere to be seen. I wondered whether he had run out of questions or was caught up in doing something else.

There are a few bamboo huts on the ashram campus. Some children study inside these huts, counsellors conduct their sessions here as well. I saw Sohan sitting inside a hut. His body language had changed completely. Happiness had drained away from him and he was crying as if he had no energy left for anything. I was shocked to see him that way.

I knew that he had no more questions for me; now it was my turn to ask questions.

'Who is the villain?' I asked.

He continued to weep without replying.

'Don't cry. Let's go watch a movie. Don't think too much.'

He did not speak.

So I sat with him holding him close. Suddenly he burst out into loud sobs. I decided to let him cry his sorrow out. After a while he stopped crying and sat lost in thought. Then he started talking and words flowed from him as if a dam had burst.

Like many runaway children, the home was the villain in Sohan's life too.

'I am sorry, uncle, I lied to you. My parents are alive and I have a younger sister, Aiswarya. My house is just as I had described earlier. But my grandmother lives with my uncle in a house near ours. She works in other people's houses and she taught me how to behave.

'My father Gopal Das works in an LPG gas agency. He delivers gas cylinders. My mother Radhi works in a garment company. She works all the time. She gets up very early in the morning and starts cooking. My father has to leave for work by 8. She packs lunch for him. My mother goes to work by 9. My father comes home drunk every evening and the fights begin. He wasn't like this. He used to come home early and ask me about my school and he would play with Aiswarya. We would eat dinner together and watch TV. We went to the movies on Sundays. At times I would go to the temple with my grandmother. My father was my hero. He taught me to ride a cycle, he even promised to buy me one to go to school. But he is very different now. He fights with my mother for no reason and beats me up. But he still loves Aiswarya. Even if he comes home drunk he brings her sweets and gifts and plays with her. I know that my mother too likes Aiswarya more than she likes me. My father spends all his money on liquor. He has no money to give us. My mother pays for everything. But he takes my mother's money too and never returns it, even if we desperately need the money. Life is very difficult at home; one day we had no food. I took ₹10 from my father's purse and bought flour. We managed with it for two days. Another day I took ₹20 from him. But my father came to know that I had taken the money and he beat me up. It was on that day that I first thought of leaving home. No one likes me, they only want Aiswarya. So why should I stay there? Mumbai was my dream city. I have always wanted to work here and live in this city. I have no one in Mumbai. I don't know either Hindi or Marathi. But I thought that I would succeed in Mumbai. I don't want a job; I want to do some business. Mumbai is the best place for that. Any business will succeed in a city that is filled with people. But I had no money to travel to Mumbai. Then the Odisha government started a scheme of giving cycles to school students. I too got ₹2600 to buy a cycle. The next day I got on a train to Howrah and from there to Mumbai. It was the first time that I was travelling by train, but I wasn't afraid. Though I was sad that I hadn't told anyone at home that I was leaving, I was sure that I would learn many new things. I would become a successful businessman and make a lot of money. Then I would go home, that was my dream. I want to give my family a lot of money. No one at home should starve. My parents and sister shouldn't cry because they have no money. I shouldn't need to steal money from my father. I believed that I had done the right thing. All these days I thought that

I would study here and start some business. But now I want to go home. I want to see everyone. They must be worried about me and I feel guilty now. I came here without telling them and I am living here comfortably, but my mother must be crying as she doesn't know where I am. Though my father creates problems, I want to go home. I want to be with my parents.'

I didn't say anything, I just held him close. He sat with me, his eyes closed, relieved that he had spoken to me. He set down the burden he had been carrying. Sohan was no longer a boy who behaved like an adult. He was a 15-year-old boy with all the anxieties of a teenager. He was a child who wanted to be with his parents, a child who wanted to go home in spite of all the problems there.

Finally I spoke, 'I am glad you told me all this. You are brave and with such courage you will definitely succeed in life. You will become a successful businessman. Anyway, let us contact your parents now.'

He smiled through his tears. I saw the brilliant smile that usually flashed across his face. He ran away to the ashram.

We decided to counsel him for three more days. That helped in erasing any negativity he harboured against his family. We were able to tell him about the difficulties he may have to face when he went back and prepared him accordingly. Within a week Sohan's parents reached the ashram. I still treasure the memory of the moment Sohan saw his parents. Though I had seen many children reuniting with their families, Sohan and his parents' reunion touched me deeply. I understood that they shared a deep bond of pure love. The three of them sat hugging without saying a word. They were weeping.

It was quite heartbreaking to watch Sohan's father. It was clear that his son's absence had torn him apart. When Sohan hugged him, his father cried loudly and held him tight. We saw a father who adored his son. We also found that Sohan was more attached to his father than to his mother. He did not let go of Sohan's hand for a long time. It was clear that he was consumed by guilt that his only son had left home because of his behaviour. He kept touching his son as if to reassure himself that he had found Sohan.

When we spoke he kept apologizing. 'I will never waste the money I earn. We are not rich, but we can live quite well with the money that we make. It is my drinking habit that destroyed everything. I won't do that again. I just want my family to be happy.'

Hearing his father Sohan felt upset. He hugged his father. 'Don't worry, Dada. I too will work. The four of us can live comfortably. I will never leave you.' He sounded determined.

He took his parents around the ashram and introduced them to everyone. He couldn't contain his happiness. Gopal Das and Radhi spoke with everyone in their broken Hindi. They were overcome with happiness to have found their son. They thanked us all at the ashram. They couldn't believe that Sohan had been taken to such a safe place in Mumbai. They were astonished to hear never-ending praises for their son.

His friends couldn't stop telling them about the two months Sohan had spent in the ashram.

Amir said, 'We die laughing when Sohan is around. He keeps us entertained all the time.'

The supervisor said, 'I have not seen a child as pleasant as Sohan. He has a positive attitude. You should be proud of him.'

Sohan realized how deeply his family had been affected by his absence. But the two months he spent away from his family brought them closer to one another. They found not only their son but also the love that had been lost in their relationship. Now they have established a very close bond, a strong connection to each other. The days of poverty and sorrow are behind them, the future is good, I was sure.

When he said goodbye, he hugged me and cried and then smiled again. I had not thought that it would be so difficult to say goodbye to him.

'Call me or send a message. Keep in touch. I want to know what you are doing.'

He promised to stay in touch. 'I will tell you about how I am, you must tell me what the stock market is like.'

'You must always be positive in your outlook, just the way you were while you were in the ashram. Whatever happens in life do not change your attitude. Your biggest plus point is your positive nature. Don't ever lose that.'

He had come to us three years ago. He still calls or texts every week and asks me about the stock market. He is pursuing a graduate programme now, and working part-time as a delivery boy for an online app.

His enthusiasm to start a business is still strong. He has no qualms about working hard to achieve his ambition.

I am sure about one thing. He will achieve his dream. Children like Sohan are very rare. Very few people can remain positive even while facing difficulties. He has a clear notion about what he wants. He will get what he wants and he will touch many lives in the course of his journey. His brilliant smile will light up the world around him. The same smile that I had seen when I first met him.

The Dreamer

December had crossed its third week. It was quite cold. The children of the ashram had started preparations for Christmas. Coloured paper bits were becoming stars and the Christmas tree was growing with flowers and berries. The ashram compound looked like a galaxy. I was helping the children with decorations.

It was then that Gargi and the team reached the ashram. They were our volunteers. She opened the door of the vehicle and got down with a big cloth bag. Behind her was a small figure peeking out of a blanket. Everyone went to the veranda.

'Rahul, this is Hari Uncle.' Gargi introduced us.

He looked at me and smiled. It was a divine smile. He stood like a priceless Christmas gift someone had sent us.

Though he was 12 he looked like an 8-year-old.

When our team saw him, he was sitting on a rusted chair near the tea shop in the railway station all by himself. When they noticed him sitting there for a long while, our team approached him. It seemed as if he were confident that someone would come to fetch him. He had an old cloth bag and a bottle of water with him. It was clear that he hadn't come to the railway station alone. He had begun to shiver from the cold and Gargi covered him with a blanket. She gave him hot tea and biscuits. Even as he was sipping the tea he looked elsewhere expecting to see someone. Our team stayed with him for a while. Then they understood that he had been abandoned. We have seen such cases before.

They asked him where he was coming from and who had brought him here. He merely smiled in his unique way. He gradually realized that he was waiting in vain. Then he told the team that his name is Rahul, he is 12 years old and is from Uttar Pradesh. He was willing to go with them to the ashram.

Apart from the smile that lit up the ashram, Rahul did not communicate with us. Our doctor examined him carefully. He had no wounds on his body and there was no evidence of sexual abuse. We were quite relieved to know that. But we couldn't imagine how anyone could have abandoned him on a platform.

Apart from telling us that his parents were dead and that he had no relatives, Rahul did not give us any information about himself. He was one of the most peaceful children I had seen. His clothes and his bag were very cheap and old. But there was something about the way he took care of his belongings and the way he dressed neatly that told us that he was a well-brought-up child.

Though he was 12, people at the ashram treated him as though he was the youngest child there.

One day our supervisor said, 'Whenever I see him I feel like running around and playing with him. I have seen many children but there is something very special about Rahul. Something magical.'

He has such a lovely smile. Even when playing football I have stood looking at the way he smiles forgetting the game,' said 14-year-old Raihan who had been Rahul's guardian and trainer ever since he came to the ashram.

To be honest, I thought of adopting him and taking him home several times. I imagined bringing him up with lots of love and care, giving him a good education and emotional support. Why did I feel that Rahul was different from the other children I had rescued? Why did I want to take him home? Who was he? Who had abandoned him?

I felt that behind his beatific smile lay a world of sorrow. One day he asked Raihan whether he could earn ₹2500 by working somewhere. When Raihan asked him why he wanted a job, Rahul did not reply.

One day I saw him sitting apart from the others, his face filled with sadness. But his posture told me that he didn't want anyone near him. I decided to leave him alone. Only time would break his silence.

Once I saw him drawing on a piece of paper, but clearly his mind was somewhere else. His friends were away at school. Then he began colouring the picture. He picked up a coloured pencil and began to colour it, then he discarded it and picked up another pencil. I observed him staring into the horizon and sighed. I couldn't bear to see his distress. I went up to him and pulled up a chair.

'Rahul, what are you doing?'

Without looking up he said, 'I am colouring this picture.'

'You look sad. Is it because your friends are at school? Don't worry, we will send you to school soon.'

He looked up at me at that moment, his eyes brimming with tears. 'I want to go home and see my grandmother. She will be sad as I am not with her.'

That was the first time he had spoken about his home from his heart.

'Don't worry, I will take you to your grandmother,' I said.

He lay his head on my lap and wept for a long while.

'You must tell me where your house is and your grandmother's name. Only then we can take you home. You must tell me why you left home.'

He started to speak, but he couldn't tell me clearly why he had left home. The days were monotonous. Only his grandmother was at home. His parents had died. Three cows, four to five goats and some hens—this was all they had. His grandmother sold milk and eggs to make ends meet. She sent him to school. He helped his grandmother with her chores. He had no friends. His grandmother taught him to dress neatly and treat people with respect. But he was bored. He felt that a better life waited for him. They couldn't even find the money to repair their house. Even as his grandmother showered him with love, he felt helpless as he couldn't help her.

One day his father's friend Balwant visited them. He was working in Mumbai. He asked Rahul's grandmother about their problems. He offered to get Rahul a job in Mumbai. But his grandmother refused—she wanted him to study and pass his exams before getting a job.

He couldn't sleep that night and lay thinking about Balwant's offer. He imagined getting a job in Mumbai, making money and helping his grandmother.

The next morning when he spoke to his grandmother about working in Mumbai, she scolded him.

Then he went to meet Balwant and told him that he wanted to work in Mumbai. Initially Balwant refused but Rahul begged until he relented. He told Rahul to meet him at the railway station the next day and he would take him to Mumbai.

That is how he left home. Throughout the journey to Mumbai he kept worrying about his grandmother. She had no other relatives. He was sure that she would be very upset that he had left home. His only solace was that Balwant had told his grandmother that he would be able to earn ₹2500 per month in Mumbai. It was a big amount and he was sure that his grandmother's problems would ease if he began to earn. But when they reached Mumbai railway station everything went awry. Balwant looked scared. He asked Rahul to sit near the tea shop and gave him a bottle of water. He left the boy there promising to come back soon.

'Balwant Uncle didn't come back, and then Gargi aunty came.'

My eyes filled with tears when I heard his story. I didn't want him to see me cry so I held him tight. I told him that we would find his grandmother soon.

Her name is Mukta Devi. She lived in Barouli, near Kaushambi, in Uttar Pradesh. The police in Kaushambi and an organization involved in children's welfare had agreed to help us trace Rahul's grandmother.

Two days later a volunteer called us. They had found Mukta Devi. She spoke to me over the telephone.

'Son.' Her voice touched me in a way I cannot explain.

I could feel tears gather in my eyes. 'Don't worry, Rahul is safe with us. He wants to come home.' Before I could finish what I was saying, his grandmother said, 'Son, take care of him please. I am coming over. I have been so worried about him.'

I could feel the love and kindness in her voice. She sounded as if she had found a treasure she had lost.

'Mother, you don't need to come here. You can send someone, or we will bring him to you. Don't travel in this cold weather at your age.'

'That isn't a problem. I will come. Don't let him go.'

I told Rahul that his grandmother was coming to take him home. He stood still for a moment and then burst into tears. Then the divine smile reappeared on his face.

The next day his grandmother called saying that she would leave in two days. She again requested us to take good care of him.

She took a week to reach Mumbai. Gargi brought her to the ashram. Rahul was waiting for her. He ran to her and hugged her. She held him close for a long while. It was as if Rahul had disappeared into the depths of her love.

She stayed with us for a few days. Rahul took her around the ashram. He was always by her side. Her son and daughter-in-law—Rahul's parents—had been killed in a shooting incident in a nearby village. Rahul was only two years old then. From that day his grandmother had looked after Rahul.

'I sold two goats to buy the ticket to Mumbai. That is why it took me a week get here,' she said in the course of our conversations. I was shocked. We knew that they depended on these goats for a living. We had told her that we would bring Rahul over, but she had sold the goats to come and fetch him. I was overcome with emotion when she said, 'If the ticket had been more expensive, I would have sold the cow as well.'

Then we knew the origin of Rahul's divine smile. It was a lamp lit by the light of his grandmother's love.

We gave them some money to buy a few goats and cows. We told Rahul to focus on his studies.

Even now I receive a call every month. 'Son' she calls me, her voice full of light, brightening my entire day.

The Billionaire's Son

Like we found many other children our staff found Amir too at Chhatrapati Shivaji Terminus. Anyone could notice him. He looked very different from children we find at railway stations who have run away from home. He was expensively dressed. His clothes, shoes and watch were branded. He carried an expensive-looking bag. He behaved as if he had come for a vacation to Mumbai. Amir was a 14-year-old boy quite fluent in Hindi and English. He only told us that he belonged to Guntur.

He had an attractive smile and was a good conversationalist. But he was silent when asked about his parents. After completing the formalities at the police station, he was brought to the ashram. It was as if he had been waiting to escape from home. He was eager to see everything and behaved as though he had come to spend his vacation with us. He quickly settled down with us. It was clear that he led a much-disciplined life and had never lacked anything. He was quite innocent.

The ashram and the children were a huge source of entertainment for Amir. He would wake up early in the morning and offer prayers to Allah. Then he would go to the study room and help the children with their work. He was very enthusiastic. As he spoke English well, the other children too wanted to speak like him. He agreed to teach them. It seemed as if Amir had opened a tuition centre at the ashram. He taught them both in the morning and evening.

He was very good at maths and could solve complicated problems easily. Initially the other children used to test his mathematical skills. He was good at science as well. He had answers to all their questions. Though he never spoke about himself in the beginning, after he began teaching the children he started to open up. But he never divulged any details. I decided to give him time to get acquainted with the ashram. I felt with time he would tell us all about himself.

The children are free to explore the ashram and enjoy themselves. Some of them open up in a couple of days, some take weeks and some children start talking only after a month or so. Then they speak frankly with us. They tell us about their fears and anxieties. They mostly tell us the truth, though some children may not tell us everything, especially if they have been sexually abused. But some children speak about themselves in detail too.

We didn't force Amir to talk. We never put down any rules for him. We gave him the freedom to do whatever he wanted to do. I felt he was enjoying the space we had given him without intruding. He taught English, science and maths like an expert teacher. He was very patient and explained in great detail. Though he was in class 8, he had the knowledge of a boy who was in class 10.

One morning I saw Amir after he had finished teaching. 'You seem to be prepared to face the board exam that you need to write in two years' time,' I told him.

His response was swift. 'Uncle, I am telling you the truth. My sister didn't do too well in the NEET exam and couldn't get into any IITs. The results came out three months ago and my mother hasn't spoken to her since then. My mother told her that she will speak to her only after she improves her score and gets into an IIT next year. My sister isn't even interested in studying at an IIT, but what can we do?'

Amir smiled at me and then dived into the crowd of children, into a world of games. It was as though he had thrown a firecracker at me. It was a conversation about a piece of his life without a beginning or an end. I saw that he had gained the courage to talk frankly. It was time to ask him about his home. He seemed ready to talk. But he was throwing a challenge at me in a playful manner. I decided to stay back and have lunch with him and talk to him after that.

As I grew up in Kerala, a state that gave a lot of importance to education, I knew the pressure parents put on their children to do well in their studies. But what Amir had said made me think. Many children dream of studying in an IIT, most parents too cherish this dream. But I wondered how Amir's mother could stop speaking to her daughter for so long. Families are quite strange. Unconditional love at times is just an idyllic dream.

Fourteen-year-old Amir belonged to Guntur in Andhra Pradesh. Guntur is an important centre for education in India. It may be the only place in the world having the maximum number of postgraduates. One in every two people we meet on the street would be a postgraduate and the other would be a student in a professional college. A large number of colleges are present and students from different states of India come to study in Guntur. The people here give priority to education. Even though they are not interested, many students here aim to clear either JEE or NEET. Coaching centres have mushroomed across Guntur. While people usually boast about their luxury cars or huge houses, people here talk about the PhDs, MTechs and MBAs their children have done, or they talk about the coaching centres for Civil Services Examinations.

I sat with Amir for lunch. I asked about the chilli farms in Guntur. He told me, 'No one is interested in cultivating chillies now; their main occupation is educating their children.' I laughed out loud when he said this. I invited him for a conversation after lunch; he was eager to talk as I had laughed at his previous joke. On the way to a bamboo hut I asked him, 'Is your mother the problem?'

'I am very scared of her. My knees tremble when I see her. I don't have the courage to speak with her. She talks and I listen. She decides what I should study and when.'

He said this almost as if he were talking to himself. He wasn't playful now. He spoke very clearly like he was delivering a speech. We sat down.

'My father is better than her. It's not that he doesn't get involved in my studies; he does! But he doesn't get angry like my mother. He knows every single detail about our studies. Even when he comes home very late he comes to check on my sister and me. He looks at what we are reading and enquires about what we did in class. He asks us how much we scored on the weekly test. He wants to know everything that happens in school. He asks us about the chapter we're currently at in school and whether we have revised our lessons for the next test. He wants to know how many marks my classmates scored. I don't know why everyone is so anxious about education. Perhaps it is because we live in Guntur. There are a large number of colleges and universities there. People there are hungry for degrees. We even have students from abroad.' He stopped and looked at me.

'My family is quite well known there. We are rich. My father runs a huge construction business and he is always busy. I have seen loving families in movies, but our family isn't like that. My parents constantly ask us to study. They don't want to know anything else about me. They have huge expectations from us. Aksa, my sister, is least interested in pursuing engineering. But my mother decided that Aksa will join IIT. Coaching began when she was in class 8. I can't tell you how angry and upset my mother was when the results were announced. She was so angry that I tried to hide from her. All hell broke loose when she found out my sister hadn't done well enough to get admission to an IIT. She hasn't spoken to Aksa since then. She has decided my future too. I have started going to coaching classes. I now have time only to write exams; exams in school, exams at the coaching centre and exams in the tuition class. My mother doesn't just ask me about my marks—she wants to know how my classmates did in the exam. She wants to know how many students did better than I did, and who the topper is. If I score 99, she wants to know if anyone got 100. She isn't happy that I scored 99; she scolds me for losing one mark. If I am not in the top three she beats me. There are various types of punishments. She only talks in terms of 100 per cent and toppers. Anything below that is bad.

'Now I realize that all I did in my school was to try and please my parents. I had an exam every day. I had to study, revise and practise for the exam. I never had time to play. Would you believe that since this year began I have never had the time to go to the school ground with my friends? The car and driver will be waiting for me when school is over. I go home, eat and go to the tuition centre. I come home at night and sit down to study. I have tuition in the morning too, before school. On Saturday and Sunday I have coaching classes.

'My friends never come over to play. I have many cousins but no one comes to stay at my place. They know my mother well. My parents throw parties regularly for friends and their relatives. But my sister and I cannot attend these parties. They tell the guests that we are studying. We are allowed to greet the guests, then we have to go upstairs and study. I feel I am a prisoner in my own home. The only difference is that I get good food and other facilities. Aksa doesn't mind sitting in her room all day long. There is a playground right next to my house where all my friends play. On holidays they start playing cricket and football in the morning. I too used to go there during holidays till last year. Everything changed when I started class 8. Now I can only watch my friends play from my window. I long to be with them but my mother won't allow me to go. I was waiting for the Diwali vacation thinking I would get time to play. But my mother had prepared a vacation timetable for me consisting of tuition, revision and tests. Everything was the same. I felt like crying when I saw this. Wasn't there an end to this?

'The day after Diwali, my mother went to attend a function with her friends. I was studying since morning. I had worked out maths problems more than a hundred times. I could hear the noise from the playground. My friends were gearing up to play football. It had been so long since I had joined them. I wanted to be with them. I slipped out without anyone seeing me. Before I could think about what I was doing I had reached the playground, sweating profusely. I felt I had reached another world. It had been so long since I had played with my friends. I had even forgotten the pleasure of playing games.

'I felt energized after playing with them for two hours. I went home feeling happy, but my mother was waiting for me at the door. The moment she saw me she started scolding me. She wouldn't stop. She told me that I couldn't leave the house without her permission. Usually, I remain silent when my mother shouts at me. I am terrified of her. But on that day I shouted back at her. She was furious. She ordered me to go and study. I retorted that I would go out to play every day during the vacation. The fight went on till night. She slapped me. My sister was scared. My father was away that night or he too would have scolded me.

'This was the first quarrel at home after Aksa's results had been declared. But as she didn't say anything, only my mother's voice was heard that day. I told my mother that I wouldn't study the whole day. What would happen if I lost a couple of marks? Would I be branded an idiot if I didn't come first in class? I could appear for the entrance exams only four years later. Why should I work like this now?

'At night sitting alone in my room I thought that my thoughts would drive me mad. They couldn't treat me like this. I didn't want to continue studying after being scolded so harshly. I walked up and down in my room, not knowing what to do. I could stop studying and fail my exams as revenge, but my mother would get angrier. If I slacked in class the teachers would inform my parents. Then the fights would begin again. I couldn't think of facing my mother's anger again. If I went out to play she would start scolding me.

'I felt I had to do something. I couldn't sleep that night. I was fed up with studying, but I didn't know what I should do. The idea of leaving home struck me then. If I went away then I would be free from my mother's scoldings. No studies or exams would bother me. I could live peacefully. It is because I lived at home that my mother shouted at me; if I left home she wouldn't be able to do that. I was thrilled to think about leaving home. I wondered why I hadn't thought about it before. It was a risk, but I thought that I would be able to handle it. I started planning from that moment.

'Could I travel alone? I had money with me as I had no opportunity to spend my pocket money. I received money as gifts, and this Diwali I had received a lot of pocket money. I thought it would be enough to find a place to stay and for food. Even as I was wondering where I could go, I knew I had to go to Mumbai. I had been to Mumbai a couple of years ago on a vacation with my parents. I had liked the city the moment I set foot there and had decided then that I would go back to Mumbai. No one would trouble me in that bustling city. No one would pester me to study, there wouldn't be any tuition or coaching. I decided to stay in Mumbai for a few days and then think what I'd do next.

'I knew how to purchase a ticket and got on a train. As Guntur is full of colleges, there are so many students at the railway station that no one pays attention to a student who is travelling alone. As I am tall, the man who gave me the ticket didn't guess that I was only 14. Once I got on the train I would be alright. My excitement mounted.

'I decided to act the next day itself. I had tuition in the morning. I used to go by car. The railway station was on the way to the tuition centre. I knew the area well. I would have to hang around till my driver left.

'I knew that the train to Mumbai was at 9 a.m. I would have covered half the distance before they found out I was missing. I packed a few clothes and snacks instead of books in my bag. I put a purse with money inside the bag. I did not carry a single book. I wouldn't study for a few days.'

He ended his story. He was very disturbed. I sat with him silently. My mind was flooded with thoughts. This was a clear violation of children's rights. How could parents treat their children like this? Getting good marks and admission into IITs are not the most important things in life. Childhood is precious. It is sad that parents destroy their children's childhood for the sake of entrance exams.

I didn't know what to tell Amir. What he said was true. I told him that we needed to think over such serious matters. We shook hands as adults.

Two weeks passed. I saw that he was enjoying life away from the pressure of exams and schoolwork. I spoke to him regularly and our counsellors had daily sessions with him. We told him that he hadn't done any wrong by running away from home and that he needn't feel guilty about it.

We treated Amir as an adult when we spoke to him. I even presented a few problems to him and asked for his help. He was able to think analytically and he spoke to me like a friend giving me his opinion. Then I got the courage to discuss his troubles with him as my doubts.

His parents would be anxious about him. We should let them know that he was safe. His family would be upset not knowing where he was. Strange things may happen at home. His parents may have been wrong to force him to study so hard, but they had the right to know where he was. Whether he wanted to go back and resume his studies were matters that could be discussed later. These were the doubts I raised during our conversation.

I told him one thing clearly—family was very important. It was fortunate that he had a home to go back to and parents who wanted him. Not everyone was so lucky. Problems at home also make children run away. But they want to go back too, especially if they get an opportunity. A house isn't just a house.

He listened carefully. He was lost in thought for

nearly a week after this. He asked me many questions with equanimity. He wanted to know about the children who had gone home from the ashram; he also wanted to know if they could be in touch with us. But he was troubled by how his parents would treat him. So at times he would tell me, 'I don't want to go back. Life will be worse than before. I will have to take my mother's permission for everything. My parents will be very angry with me. They might even hire security to take me to the tuition centre. It will be so shameful. No, I can't think of going back. You don't know my mother. When she gets angry it is impossible to be near her. She creates so much noise. She screams, and it is not easy to deal with her. Even if I score good marks she will blame me for missing a month of school. She doesn't know how to love.'

We spoke to him for a long time. We could understand his fear. It was only natural for him to be anxious about the way his parents would react. I told him, 'You are only 14; you are a smart boy and good at studies. You will reach great heights, but you need your parents' support now. You can stay here and study or you can stay somewhere else. But we have to discuss this with your parents. Let them come. I will convince them. Your parents will treat you well, don't worry. They would have realized their mistake after you left home. They will be kinder to your sister too. Your running away would have created a positive change in them.'

After many such conversations Amir gave us his father's number. I called him. I began the conversation by telling him that Amir was safe. I could hear the relief and surprise in his father's voice. We gave him our address. I told him that his son was safe with us and he could come over and meet him. I guessed his father was in shock. He didn't ask to speak to Amir.

I told him that he could come and take his son home or we could send him over after going through some formalities at the police station. But things happened at a speed we hadn't expected.

Within 5 minutes of speaking to Amir's father, all the phones in the ashram began to ring. People were ringing from Andhra Pradesh and Mumbai. The Guntur police rang us wanting to know if Amir was with us. A senior police officer from Andhra called immediately after this. Then it was the turn of the Mumbai police. We wondered if the entire police force had taken up this case.

We had rescued thousands of children and sent them home safely, but we couldn't understand why there was so much of interest in this case.

When the next call came from the police, I asked the officer, 'Why are so many people calling us? The minute Amir gave us his phone number we contacted his father. His parents can take him home. We have many years of experience in helping such children. We have been running this foundation for years now. You can ask anyone about us. Children are safe here till they go back home. We want the children to return to their homes, we don't hold them back here unlawfully. You can speak to the children here if you want.'

After a minute the officer replied, 'Don't you know who this boy is?'

I didn't understand the question.

I said, 'Amir just gave me his father's phone number. I don't know Guntur well. Who is Amir's father? Is he a VIP? A politician? Or a police officer? I don't understand.'

He wasn't a movie actor I was sure. Perhaps a director or a producer? Amir had told me that his father had a construction business.

I asked, 'Who is Amir's father?'

'A businessman—a billionaire businessman.'

Though Amir had told us he was from a rich family, we hadn't guessed that they were that wealthy. A billionaire's son had left home and behaved like an ordinary boy who helped the children of the ashram. Wonders will never cease. Families are strange.

We got more information about Amir's father from the police. He was a real estate king. He was a well-known builder not just in Guntur, but in the whole of Andhra Pradesh. He was a man who had contacts with police officers, politicians and the government. No wonder the phones had been ringing constantly.

In the evening we got a call from the top-most official in Mumbai police.

'Amir's mother is here. Please make arrangements to send him home immediately.'

'Tonight? Why? She can come here and see him and take him back in the morning. We have to complete the formalities with the police.'

'No, she is insistent. You know it's not easy to convince a mother in such a situation. It's a very sensitive situation and we can't do anything about it.'

He lowered his voice, 'She suspects that you have converted Amir, she is creating a lot of trouble here.'

Converted Amir? Why were we accused of that? Was it because we called this place run by the foundation an ashram? Yet it is true that such allegations are often levelled at us. We face a lot of questions about the work we do to help children. Where do we get the money from? Who sponsors us? Why do we allow so many children to stay here? We answer all these questions quite clearly. People like to believe that we have the backing of some religious organization. Some people spread rumours that such organizations encourage religious conversion to increase their numbers.

I told him that Amir's mother need not fear anything of that sort and that she was free to meet him. She insisted on coming to the ashram immediately to meet Amir. I too thought that she may be upset by his absence and that she would be relieved when she came here and saw that he was safe. Amir was happy here. He had regained everything he had lost by focusing on his studies and was now celebrating his renewed interests and hobbies.

Amir was healthier than he had been when he came to us. Even his demeanour had changed to a livelier one once he stopped being cooped up in a room full of books. He used to climb trees, play in the soil and run around with his friends. I thought that his mother would notice all this, but what happened was very different.

A row of luxury cars and police vehicles reached the ashram. As I was away the staff showed me a live recording of what was going on. Amir's mother was fuming with anger when she got out of the car. That was enough to convince me that Amir had been telling the truth when he said he was scared of his mother. She was rude to everyone and shouted. I couldn't see any happiness on her face when she saw Amir. She behaved as if he were an appliance that she had bought from the store that hadn't been delivered.

Even when Amir came to her she did not smile or hug him. She just said, 'Get ready quickly.'

He asked softly, 'I haven't said goodbye to my friends. Can't we go in the morning?'

He was worried his mother would kick up a row. She silenced him with a look. He went in and got his bag.

She continued to question everyone around her in a raised voice. She was ordering us around without once thinking that we had kept her son safe when he reached Mumbai all alone. She acted as if we were supposed to obey her commands.

When Amir came out she asked our staff, 'How much should I pay you?'

I lost it then. I don't know what I would have said had I been in the ashram. I was furious, she had humiliated us. Our staff were also hurt.

She was putting a price on the care we had given her son. I could only think of one answer. I told my team, 'Tell her that we don't need her money and that her son is a gift from us.'

They repeated what I said.

I told them to complete the formalities and send them away as soon as possible. All the paperwork was completed in the presence of the police. As soon as the papers were signed, Amir was handed over to them. They left at the same speed that they had come in.

I felt sad that I couldn't meet Amir before he left. He had promised to contact us. It was my responsibility to find out if he was happy at home.

After a week, I got an unexpected call. It was from Amir's father. He was in Mumbai and wanted to meet me. We fixed up a convenient time to meet. We met at the office of the foundation. He had no airs of a billionaire businessman. He was a dignified, quiet man, unlike his wife. I found that he had been quite upset that Amir had run away from home. He blamed himself when he spoke.

'Things have changed a lot at home. In fact, we have changed. I haven't recovered from the shock yet. He took that step because of us and the way we treated him. It is not easy to learn that we were bad parents. All I can say is that we won't repeat our mistakes. Amir's happiness is far more important than any IIT admission.'

I felt he was truly remorseful and Amir wouldn't have to face any more problems at home. He wouldn't be forced to study all the time or come first in class. Amir's running away from home had yielded something good.

Amir's father had come after getting to know how we had helped Amir and what the Foundation did for runaway children. He said, 'Please don't misunderstand but I would like to give some money to the foundation, not because you helped my son. But for the activities of the foundation as you have to help many such children.'

I refused to accept money and reminded him that there was a lot he could do to help. 'If you want to help perhaps you could start a fund for underprivileged children. I am sure Guntur has many such children. It will be a blessing if you could help them.'

Amir's father looked at me in silence. Then he came up to me and hugged me. He was crying. I felt his tears within me. I have no words to describe such a deeply emotional experience.

After a while he said, 'Inshallah I will do that.'

That day was ten years ago. Amir and Aksa are now engineers. They are happy. Amir calls me often. He still speaks with the exuberance of a 14-year-old boy. We still remember how smart and capable he was then. We feel we were lucky to have seen him at the railway station. We were able to save not only him but also his family.

The Volunteer

It was Pooja who first noticed a 15-year-old boy searching for the exit at the railway station. He was carrying an overstuffed school bag and was wearing mismatched clothes. She pointed him out to Vijay. The boy had walked confidently across the platform but was now anxiously searching for the exit.

Pooja and Vijay, our volunteers, were on duty at the Kalyan railway station that day. They were very astute and could pick up the slightest changes in behaviour. They went up to him and greeted him. He smiled and spoke to them. He looked directly at them while speaking. His behaviour suggested that he thought he was smarter than them. His name was Govinda and he belonged to a village near Nanded. His father was a farmer.

The railway officials and our team arrived. They asked him for his ticket.

He was unfazed. He gave a speech to Pooja and Vijay.

'Do you know how poor my village is? We lead extremely difficult lives. My parents, our neighbours, my friends and their families—everyone works in the fields from early morning to evening. We work in the fields cultivating cotton, pulses or banana trees. People work like slaves. If they fall ill with fever they shiver because of poverty. I don't want a future there. My classes are over. I have nothing to do there. I have often thought of coming to Mumbai. I am sure I can find employment here. My future is here.' Our team gave him water and biscuits. They tried to explain the situation to him. 'You have travelled without a ticket. You are a minor and so the law will not allow you to work. You will be taken to the juvenile court of justice and they will send you to a shelter for children. Then they will send you back home. You are lucky you didn't fall into the hands of any gang that kidnaps children and turns them into beggars. Children who come here alone become victims to many cruelties.'

When he realized the gravity of the situation, he agreed to come with us. We gave his name and other available details to the police and lodged an FIR. After that, we took him to the Swami Vivekananda Manparivartan Kendra at Mamnoli. He was gazing at the city throughout the journey to the ashram. It was as if he had reached home after wandering around for days.

He had only cheap magazines with colourful illustrations in his bag; he didn't even have a spare set of clothes to change into. But from the very first day, he adapted to life in the ashram.

We begin our day at six. Govinda woke up much earlier than that. He completed the tasks his teacher had assigned with enthusiasm. He read his books carefully and helped in the kitchen. He cleaned the ashram premises and worked on our farm.

On interacting with him, our counsellors felt that if he were sent home he would run away again. So we didn't probe for details. We decided to wait till he expressed a desire to return to his family.

He had no other possessions except for the cheap magazines. I once went through them. They were in Hindi and English and had colourful pictures of urban life. When I asked him about the magazines he told me that he hadn't travelled beyond Nanded but had always wanted to live in a city and find work there. When he flipped through these magazines he felt as though he were walking through the streets of a city. He didn't find a single person in his village who shared his dream. He only spoke to his mother about this. He always spoke to her about huge cities.

'Why did you choose Mumbai?' I asked him.

'Ganga Ram bhai worked in Mumbai. I used to go and meet him when he came to our village. He told me that people in Mumbai led much better lives than the villagers did.'

'Where in Mumbai does Ganga Ram live?' I asked.

But his silence told me that he wouldn't give me any further information.

He was quite involved in his studies and never indicated that he wanted to go home during his meetings with the counsellors. He behaved as though he had been born and brought up in Mumbai. He seemed confident that no one would come looking for him. So I decided to look for a school for him in Mumbai.

But the day after I made the decision, Govinda's father Ravindra appeared at the ashram. He looked fatigued. He was wearing shabby clothes, had no slippers and his heels had cracks.

'I don't know who saw whom first, but they are still hugging.' Vijay called me from the ashram to announce the new development.

I went to the ashram the next day. I wanted to meet Ravindra. I wanted to know more about their family. Though Govinda hadn't told us much about his home I sensed that he came from a family that didn't share a strong bond. I used to have serious conversations with the parents of the children we rescued. During such sessions I used to feel that I was doing fieldwork for research in social science.

Vijay reported information regarding Ravindra.

He came from a remote village near Nanded in

the Marathwada region in Maharashtra. His name was Ravindra Chawan. The villages in Nanded were known for farming. But the torrential rain during August and the sweltering heat in April and May created huge troubles for the farmers. Ravindra had sold his farm in Ardhapur and bought land in Nanded. Nanded was the second-largest district in Maharashtra. He thought if he lived near this place he could give his children good education. The greatest dream Ravindra, who had dropped out of school in class 5, was that his son Govinda would pass his exams and get an office job. Though he had great dreams about his son, he never spoke with Govinda about them. He had never once touched his son lovingly. Not just Ravindra, no one in the village was given to such gestures of affection. But the villagers used to make their children work on the farm and at home. This was not a practice Ravindra and his wife Sita followed. They watched with pride as their son flipped through the colourful magazines. I asked Vijay whether Ravindra had told him about any quarrel at home that may have persuaded Govinda to leave. Vijay said he hadn't had the time for such a detailed conversation. Now the father and son had gone to look at the cows in the ashram.

I went to the barn near the ashram. We got milk that we needed from the cows in the ashram. I saw that Ravindra was bathing the cows and Govinda was helping him. They were laughing at some joke. Vijay had told me there was no warmth in their relationship, but all that had changed in a day. When he saw me, Govinda ran to me and caught my hand. It was the first time he was touching me. I felt a light breeze had kissed my hand. Ravindra took off his turban and wiped his hands on it. He came to me and wished me, 'Ram, Ram!' He folded his hands. I too folded my hands. He behaved as though he had been working in the barn for years.

'Father and son seem to be deep in conversation.'

'Saab, I couldn't believe it when I saw him yesterday. He has changed so much. The frown on his forehead has disappeared. He hugged me.' The father sounded overjoyed.

'It's the first time he has spoken to me like this and the first time he is helping me with my work. Everything has changed, saab.'

'Why did you never talk to each other before?' I asked Ravindra.

'I never called him to help me. I loved to watch him read and study. I wanted him to get a job. Farming doesn't earn money. I was going to speak to him because the week before he left, he sat brooding at home.'

Hearing this Govinda slipped into silence.

'What was bothering you?' I asked Govinda.

Though he turned to look at me, his expression didn't

change. His eyes filled with tears but he took care to hold them back. I felt the pain he was going through. I knew he wouldn't cry when his father was by his side.

I asked him to come for a walk with me. He held my hand as we walked. He became a small child and told me why he had left his home.

He had been bored with life in the village. He became obsessed with the thought of leaving the place. When he found that he couldn't get rid of the urge to leave he told his mother that he wanted to visit Hazur Sahib. This was a place sacred to the Sikh community, which was 40 km away from Nanded. His mother ignored his request initially as there was no money. But he kept pestering her. When Ravindra came home at night, Sita told him about their son's demand. Ravindra immediately agreed. He said their son had never asked for anything before and told his wife to take Govinda and visit the place as he did not have money for the three of them to travel. Govinda was very happy in Hazur Sahib; he was excited to see different types of people and many factories. He kept comparing life in Hazur Sahib to the dull life in his village. But his mother couldn't understand what he was trying to say. When they got back he told his mother that he would not stay in the village. He wanted to go to Mumbai and request Ganga Ram to get him a job. She became angry and told him to get a job after he completed his studies. He retorted that he would study after he made some money. She didn't reply. Gradually, Govinda lost interest in everything around him; he had only one desire—to leave home.

Even now he wasn't guilty that he had run away from home, but he was deeply touched that his father had come all this distance just to see him.

I told him that I appreciated him opening up to me and not only that, he had been communicating with his father as well. So I told him to show his father our ashram and that I would talk to Ravindra after that. I told him not to worry and left.

Ravindra was impressed by the activities of our ashram. He stayed with us for two days. For us it was the first time that a parent was staying at the ashram, making an effort to understand the way we functioned and working with us wholeheartedly. But what was amazing was the way Govinda's father had discovered our ashram.

He had noticed the change that had come over his son when he returned from Hazur Sahib. He spoke about it to his wife and he decided to talk to Govinda. He came home early that day to speak to his son but was too late. He wasn't there. The corner where Govinda kept his school bag was vacant and his magazines also were missing. The house felt empty. He went around the neighbourhood looking for his son. The neighbours consoled him saying that the boy must be playing somewhere. Time went by and night set in without any news of the boy. Sita started weeping. Ravindra and his friends started searching for Govinda.

At dawn, Ravindra went to the police station. He wept when he told them that his son was missing. The policeman said, 'Children who run away from home come back a few days later.' But he didn't return. Ravindra went to the police station every day, his eyes tired and body taut with worry.

'What will we do if he doesn't come home? Where will I go to find him?' he asked them.

Without looking up, a policeman said, 'If he doesn't come back within a week, we will file a missing complaint.'

Ravindra couldn't face his wife. She blamed him for everything. Unable to bear his grief, he sat in a corner of his hut. He kept thinking about his son and cursed himself as he felt guilty.

Days passed. Ravindra stopped working on his farm. He only left his house to go to the police station. This became a daily sight for the villagers. The policemen became impatient with him. They spoke to him harshly when he asked about his son, 'We will close the missing case. We don't have a budget to advertise and travel to find your son.'

When he realized that money was needed to find his

son, Ravindra became desperate. He had no money and as the crops had failed, he was in debt. He lost hope in the police and walked away from the police station. He decided to talk to someone about finding Govinda. He went to his son's school. He met a teacher, Madhav Patil. The villagers sought his advice for everything from getting a loan for agricultural purposes to a marriage proposal. Thinking that the teacher would have a solution Ravindra poured his heart out to him.

Madhav Patil said, 'Govinda must have gone to Mumbai. Boys of his age dream of that city. There is a train that leaves our village every night for Mumbai.'

Mumbai? Though the city was just a night's journey away, Ravindra had never been there. He hadn't even been to Ardhapur in fifteen years. How could he find his son in Mumbai? He had heard about the busy streets and the slums in Mumbai. Not knowing what his son would be doing there, he started weeping.

Madhav Patil said, 'You can take the train tonight itself, or get a ride on a truck. Once you get there don't waste your time looking for him on the streets, go to the police stations. There are organizations in Mumbai that give information to the police about children who have run away from home.'

He wanted nothing more than to find his son. He boarded the train to Mumbai that night and got down at the last stop. He hadn't thought of where he would go or to whom he would speak. The busy station bewildered him. He asked a tea vendor where the police station was. The man asked him which police station he wanted to go to. He replied, 'Mumbai Police Station.'

The man asked Ravindra whether it was his first time in Mumbai. Ravindra did not reply. The man felt sorry for Ravindra and told him the way to the toilet and to the police station. He added that there were many police stations in Mumbai.

The crowd at the police station was huge. He didn't have the courage to speak to anyone. He stood there till afternoon, then he saw a policeman who was writing down complaints. He somehow gathered courage and approached the policeman. When the officer asked him why he had come Ravindra said that his son was missing.

'When did the boy go missing?'

'Two months ago.'

The policeman angrily asked him why he had waited so long to file a complaint. He became angrier when Ravindra told him that he had come from a distant village. He asked Ravindra why he hadn't filed a complaint at the village police station. Hearing this Ravindra started weeping loudly. That is when the policeman began to listen to his story. He felt sympathy for the poor man who was desperately searching for his son. He advised

Ravindra to enquire at Dadar Police Station or the children's home in Matunga and go to Kalyan if he didn't get information from these places. Ravindra spent the next four days going to these places. He was tired out as he survived on tap water and slept on the streets, but he did not give up hope. He begged for help from the police officers. He walked 50 km to get to Kalyan from Matunga.

He spoke about his woes to several policemen. One of them took pity on him and spoke to his colleagues about the missing boy. They checked the computer files on missing children. Within half an hour they located Govinda who was in our ashram. They got the information that he had been with us for two months now.

Would Ravindra have been able to locate his son easily if he had offered a bribe? The data could have been easily accessed from any police station. When one thinks of the nightmarish days Ravindra and his wife went through, one cannot but criticize the police force who are supposed to help and protect the citizens.

I would say that it wasn't due to the efforts of the police force that Ravindra was able to track his son—it was sheer luck.

'I never thought that I could do all this. Many of the children in the neighbourhood have run away from home. Life in the village is really difficult. Parents hope that their children will come home one day. But I couldn't do that. I couldn't wait at home hoping that he would come back for Navratri or Diwali. I may have been a bad father, and I may not have tried to understand my son, but that doesn't mean that I would abandon him. I had to find him.' Ravindra told me once, explaining why he had gone through such hardships trying to find his son. His words were firm and filled with passion. I felt great respect for him. I felt that I was standing before a wise sage and peace filled my soul.

As a man who had spent his life working in the soil, Ravindra easily understood the strong bond the people of the ashram had with nature. Along with his son, Ravindra tended to the plants and trees in the ashram. He spoke about many things. The father and son came to know each other far more in the few days they spent together at the ashram than they had in the 15 years they had lived together at home. As he was not a talkative person, Ravindra couldn't communicate with his son, and Govinda too withdrew into himself. But with untold joy, we watched them break down the walls they had built around themselves.

Govinda was ready to go back home. I promised to support him in his studies and in his efforts to find a job. We told them that we could help Ravindra too.

But in his soft voice brimming with respect, he said,

'Saab, it is my turn now. You have helped me find my son, allow me to pay my debt.'

I wondered what this man who had wandered on foot for days seeking his son had to tell me. I stood before him with respect, not taking my eyes off his face writ with simplicity.

This was his wish:

We should allow him to become a volunteer who helps us find missing children and take care of them.

I couldn't believe my ears. We had rescued thousands of children but this was the first time a father had expressed a desire to be a volunteer. This request from a poor farmer in a remote village in Maharashtra touched us deeply.

I understood that Ravindra's perception of children and his worldview had changed completely. I bowed before him. He was a star, a wise star.

The Soldiers

The Dongri shelter home in Mumbai functions under the direct supervision of the state government and the children's welfare organization. Boys and girls below 18 are offered a safe space there.

Mothers who are in jail can keep their children with them till they turn six years old. Children above six are sent to Dongri Shelter and Observation Home. Girls who run away from home are also allowed to stay there. Children who indirectly or accidentally get involved in criminal cases are also sent to stay there till they are 18. Voluntary organizations and the police work here, trying to send children who have run away from home back to their families. If the parents are poor, arrangements are made to send the children home with the help of the police. There are structured daily activities for the children who are brought here. For the first twenty days, orientation programmes are conducted to identify the abilities and interests of the children, then there are counselling sessions to evaluate their interests and then training is given to them in such identified areas so that they become employable. Usually children receive training in stitching, computer operation, mobile phone repair, carpentry, plumbing or electrical works.

Though I used to go with the superintendent to hold counselling sessions for girls, I spent most of my time counselling boys and doing paperwork when I went to Dongri Shelter and Observation Home. Usually the boys who come here have more complex emotions than the girls. Moreover the girls find it easier to speak to female counsellors. The superintendent took great care of the children here.

It was a usual day at Dongri Shelter and Observation Home. The number of children had increased and it was becoming difficult to pay attention to each of them. So we had decided at the board meeting to try and locate the families of these children and to send them home. I was busy doing paperwork for the same. The superintendent came in and told me, 'Hari, please speak to these girls. They are waiting outside the cabin. They insist that they want to speak to you.'

'Madam, are these the girls who want to join the army?'

She said that they were the same girls.

'Tell them that they need to be graduates or they have to pass plus two to join the army. Anyway, tell them that I will look into the matter.'

I had to complete the paperwork and rush to Swami Vivekananda Manparivartan Kendra.

The superintendent did not budge. She said softly, 'You have to meet them. They are refusing to return to their rooms. I have been telling them what you have just told me for the past week. But now they are determined. They insist on meeting you.'

The moment I agreed, three girls came into the cabin. The determination on their faces surprised me. I asked them to sit down. They kept standing and told me that they wanted to join the army. The three of them had come here for different reasons and had now become fast friends. They had made a firm decision to join the army. Amisha, Anuradha, Anitha—they stood before me like soldiers.

Amisha was from the Northeast. Her father had left her mother when Amisha was two years old. Her mother took another partner and he controlled everything in the house. She couldn't even speak to her mother in private. One day he said that Amisha could be in the circus. Neither she nor her mother had ever thought about this. They opposed his suggestion. But he had everything planned. Ignoring their protests, he sent her to a circus company in a village. She was 14 years old then. She was quite agile and soon her fame spread.

Bigger circus companies wanted her to join them. One day, without her knowledge, the circus company she had been working for sold her to a bigger one. She had to leave without even saying goodbye to her mother. The new company toured villages. She soon understood that she was a commodity that had been sold. The manager of the circus company sexually exploited her. Even though she protested, he continued to abuse her.

One day the circus company put down its tents in a village she knew. Amisha was tired of the sexual abuse she had to suffer. On the day of the inauguration she too had gone on the parade around the village with the other circus people and animals. Walking around the village disturbed her emotionally. She refused to enter the ring when she was due to perform. She was beaten up badly and went to the ring blankly.

What happened next was astonishing. She spoke to the audience about the brutalities she had faced. The people rose in anger. The manager was arrested. Amisha was sent to the Dongri shelter as part of the rehabilitation process by the juvenile board.

Anuradha was from Chennai. Her mother was Tamil and her father was Telugu. Her father died when she was a child. Her mother struggled to bring her up. When she completed her plus two, her mother found her a job in a mobile repair shop. She quickly learnt to repair mobiles and other electronic equipment. She fell in love with a man who was working in the shop. He promised to marry her. She moved in with him and shifted to another part of the town without telling her mother. But even after three months he didn't marry her. Realizing that she was being cheated, she went back to her mother. Life became difficult as she did not have a job and her mother kept blaming her for being foolish. She kept crying and slowly sank into depression.

Another young man approached her. He was her only solace. They eloped and came to Mumbai. Soon his love and kindness vanished and in a few months, he too disappeared. She was found by the police during a raid at Red Street and she was sent to the Dongri shelter.

Anitha was from a remote village in Maharashtra. Her father was a farmer and her mother too helped in the small plot of land that they owned. Her parents would return only late in the evening from the field. Anitha had to take care of her younger siblings. She had to take them to school and come back home and cook. In the evening she had to bring them back from school. She had to wash clothes and clean the house. Her chores were never-ending.

She desired to wear good clothes and jewellery and go to fancy restaurants. But her parents scolded her when she talked about all this. They couldn't understand what she wanted. One day she decided to go to Mumbai. She was running away from boredom and disappointment with her life in the village. Luckily, our volunteers spotted her at the railway station and brought her to the Dongri shelter. As she had no desire to go back she didn't give us any information about her family.

I have mentioned earlier that I don't take up the task of counselling girls. At Manparivartan Kendra we only take care of boys. There is a mafia that waits for girls who run away to Mumbai. Life becomes horrifying once a girl falls into their hands. The police and government agencies have limitations when they get involved in these matters. Such cases don't come to me personally. I am narrating the story of these girls as an experiential model.

It was easy to understand that these girls hadn't received much care or attention at home. Shouldn't parents spend some time at least with their children? Shouldn't they listen to their children? The reality is that our society doesn't pay much attention to them.

The three girls were determined to see me as they thought I was influential and would be able to help them join the army. I explained that joining the army was not as easy as joining the school. I convinced them that they needed training and would have to apply when the armed services recruit candidates. Actually I didn't know how to help them and also thought that after their sessions with the counsellors, their plans might change. I decided to give them time.

Before leaving, I asked the superintendent whether their families had been traced. She told me that Anitha had refused to provide any details and the other two girls were adamant not to return even when the centre had details of their families.

I couldn't go to Dongri for the next two weeks. But the superintendent used to call me and tell me that the girls were still determined to join the army. They had begun to get agitated as they couldn't find a way to join the forces. Meanwhile, Anitha had given them the details of her parents. Her father had been contacted and he had said that he would come to pick her up the following week.

Before I went to the Dongri shelter I enquired in detail about the process involved to join the armed forces. The three of them came to my cabin. They had covered their heads with dupattas. Though I didn't notice this, the superintendent told me they had shaved their heads in protest as they couldn't join the army.

Shocked at hearing this, I looked at them. They took off their dupattas. They had shaved off their luxuriant locks. Their eyes shone with determination beneath the shaved heads. I was at a loss for words. They were like children in their stubbornness. I spent the whole day with them explaining the process involved to join the armed forces. I got to know about the step-by-step process. They listened attentively. First they had to join school and then take special physical education classes. They must eat healthy food. They must think positively and wait patiently for the next recruitment drive. I took time to explain all this. They agreed to do as I told them. I took on the responsibility of enrolling them in schools, putting them in a hostel and finding a trainer for them.

Anitha's father came to meet her. Though he forced her to go back with him, she refused. After a few days, both parents came to see her. They spoke to her in front of the superintendent and admitted their mistake. When they realized that they had not been able to pay attention to Anitha's needs as they toiled to make ends meet, things became easier. As she had not been sexually abused and as her parents and siblings were all at home and because her parents would now pay heed to her wishes gave Anitha the courage to return home. We sent her home only after she and her parents underwent family counselling.

Amisha and Anuradha went to college for two years. Their only ambition was to join the army. Each time I saw them I understood that they were becoming stronger and more mature. Both of them were selected to join the army.

We arranged a farewell party for them. When they were abused no one helped them, but now these young women were ready to sacrifice themselves for the nation.

Though I have only this story to tell about runaway girls, I would like to underscore one thing. Girls have to be given as much attention as boys by parents and society. Girls are treated like wage-less labourers in many domains. Our society doesn't even give them the freedom to make their own choices. Girls are more determined and focused than boys. They can make significant contributions to social progress.

Most girls who run away from home have heartbreaking stories to tell. As I have not been personally involved in the rehabilitation of girls, I have not narrated their stories in this book. Our society should not hesitate to recognize that girls like Amisha and Anuradha are filled with determination and are willing to work hard. That is something that I wish to reiterate.

Acknowledgements

Firstly, I'd like to thank Resul Pookutty, who inspired me to write this book and convinced me that it was necessary to put out these stories to the world.

The next person to thank would be my dear friend Kumar Bhaskar for making this happen. I will forever be grateful for his tireless efforts and his help in bringing out this book. In fact, I am lucky to have a bunch of great friends, and would like to take this opportunity to convey my gratitude to the Nariman Point gang—Showkath, Girish, Rammohan, Prasad, Krishnadas and Rajgopal.

I would also like to thank Shri Sanjay Kelkar (MLA) for his support in all our activities at Samatol Foundation and Shri Vijay Jadhav for his passion towards reuniting runaway children with their families.

My sincere thanks also goes to my parents, who introduced me to this philanthropic world and motivated me to always help children in need. One's family is the best support system that anyone can ask for. My biggest thank you is to my family—my wife Harneet and my lovely children Karan and Aayushi—who have unfailingly stood by me and supported me in such endeavours.

Writing a book is one thing and getting it published is another. I'm glad that I have Dipti Patel (of WordFamous) as my literary agent, who has been very active in assisting me with every aspect of the book and getting Rupa Publications on board.

Lastly, I would like to acknowledge Rupa Publications—especially Dibakar Ghosh and my editor Shatarupa Dhar—for the expeditious transformation of the manuscript into this anthology of true stories.